Praise for *The Eloquence of Silence*

"*The Eloquence of Silence* is itself eloquent and quiets the restless mind. The stories and comments point to the spaciousness that is inside everything. This is the understanding that gives life joy. The thing is that Thomas Moore has a lovely, easy style; as you read the book, the world starts to slow down, the stories make a bridge, the silence goes straight into your own heart. This book is delicious. I ate it all in one sitting."

— **John Tarrant**, author of *The Light Inside the Dark: Zen, Soul, and the Spiritual Life*

"This precious book is an extraordinary journey into silence and emptiness, one that touches all aspects of life and is revelatory."

— **Rev. Joan Jiko Halifax**, abbot at Upaya Zen Center and author of *Standing at the Edge*

"I have one hand clapping (loudly) for Thomas Moore's eloquent and epicurean honoring of less, where even nothing can be plenty. This is not just a book but a crystalline conjuring of uncluttered consciousness, a compellingly lucid and often funny meditation on unsuspected portals to magic and freedom."

— **Bill Plotkin**, author of *Soulcraft* and *The Journey of Soul Initiation*

"I read Thomas Moore's book on emptiness, and I found it very full. In *The Eloquence of Silence*, Moore shows us that emptiness doesn't mean nothing or that nothing matters; rather, it exposes the great expansive significance of everything. I like the effect the book has. It will surely benefit anyone who reads it and pays attention."

— **David Chadwick**, author of *Crooked Cucumber: The Life and Zen Teaching of Shunryu Suzuki*

THE ELOQUENCE
OF
SILENCE

Also by Thomas Moore

Ageless Soul

Care of the Soul

Dark Nights of the Soul

Original Self

The Planets Within

A Religion of One's Own

Rituals of the Imagination

Soul Mates

The Soul of Christmas

The Soul of Sex

Soul Therapy

Writing in the Sand

THE ELOQUENCE
OF
SILENCE

SURPRISING WISDOM IN
TALES of EMPTINESS

THOMAS MOORE

New World Library
Novato, California

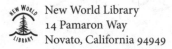

New World Library
14 Pamaron Way
Novato, California 94949

Text design by Tona Pearce Myers

Library of Congress Cataloging-in-Publication data is available.

First printing, May 2023
ISBN 978-1-60868-866-1
Ebook ISBN 978-1-60868-867-8

Printed in Canada on 100% postconsumer-waste recycled paper

New World Library is proud to be a Gold Certified Environmentally Responsible Publisher. Publisher certification awarded by Green Press Initiative.

10   9   8   7   6   5   4   3   2   1

To the musical loons of Thorndike Pond

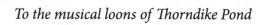

We are surrounded by a rich and fertile mystery. May we not probe it, pry into it, employ ourselves about it, a little?

HENRY DAVID THOREAU

CONTENTS

INTRODUCTION

I had just published *Care of the Soul* and was scheduled to speak about it at a small, little-known bookstore in Portland, Oregon. It was a big trip for me, the first of my career as a writer, and it was a long way from my home in New England. It was also only two weeks before my wedding, and I wore my new suit, the only one I had, having no idea how I should dress but wanting to make a good impression.

At that time, I would have been happy if my book sold a thousand copies, since I had little hope it would be a success. I had written four books previously that together had sales of about five hundred. I was sure my publisher would be disappointed in this one.

When I arrived at the store about a half hour early, I was surprised how small it was and to find that it was more of a gift shop, with a few books on scattered shelves. The owner was waiting for me alone and seemed surprised that I would make the long trip from New England just to be at his out-of-the-way shop. He told me to sit down and wait a while because people often came a little late for authors.

I sat on a wood bench in the store, only later discovering that it had just recently been shellacked, and I got stains on the back of my only suit, the one intended for my wedding. But I sat and waited. And waited. After a half hour, the time allotted for my talk, the owner suggested I go back to my hotel, since it was clear now that no one would be coming.

I wasn't too disappointed because my hopes had not been high, but I walked back to my hotel slowly, thinking that I had been right, that my kind of writing would have no takers and I'd have to get used to empty bookstores and unimpressed owners. I thought about other ways I might make a living and set about my life's work.

But the following night, at Seattle's sprawling Elliott Bay bookstore, about two hundred people showed up, noisy and excited, and I discovered that I could do stand-up comedy as part of my routine. I sold a ton of copies, and that book, *Care of the Soul*, went on to be read by millions of people all over the world.

This is a story about emptiness. Not literal zero or nothingness, but a quality that eases excessive control, literalism, or egotism in any activity. That evening of emptiness in Portland taught me not to be attached to obvious and literal success but to remain indifferent to how my work is received, to cherish my creations whether or not anyone shows up to express their approval. It was a lesson in what in Indian philosophy is known as *sunyata*, a special, deep, spiritual, and meaningful emptiness, an idea to study and contemplate, a mysterious something that is the focus of the great Heart Sutra and the many pages of theoretical writing by the sage Nagarjuna, an attitude and even a way of life that prizes detachment and an open mind.

This is a book of traditional stories and thoughts about emptiness. I draw stories from spiritual traditions, folktales, literature, and my own life, reflecting on how each relates to our daily lives. Stories of empty pots, unadorned fingers, bows without arrows, and an empty tomb hint at the great spiritual and philosophical idea of emptiness. My empty bookstore is simply one example among many.

After reading this book, you might notice ordinary instances of emptiness in every aspect of your life and see through the literal fact to the mystery, the poetry of an empty box, an empty seat at a theater, or an empty silence in a crowded room. You may allow emptiness in various forms into your life, as you wake up to unexpected sources of meaning. That is how I see spiritual emptiness: as a way to be open and awake and to take life seriously but lightly.

Emptiness is not a popular idea in modern life, which wants to fill any sign of ignorance with information and stuff the world with new products. Emptying seems useless and counterproductive, which it is, in a certain sense.

Perhaps we produce too many things and use too many words and even think too many thoughts. That empty store in Portland taught me an important lesson. I learned how to live with nothingness and carry what novelist Philip Roth called "the human stain," original sin, human imperfection. There is a power in life that will empty us out, no matter how hard we try to be perfect.

When you lose a job or a spouse or a friend, you feel the emptiness for a long time afterward, maybe forever. That emotion of loss can cover over a deeper philosophical emptying out, the discovery that life itself is often empty and that usually in emptiness you can find new life. In the dark emotions emptiness brings, you may find a hint of light.

You can learn to appreciate emptiness and make it part of your daily experience. It can give you peace and comfort, especially when life is full and active. It balances out any tendency to do too much or even to think and feel excessively.

Of course, spiritual emptiness goes much deeper. Your beliefs and values have an empty core. You can't be too attached to them or take them too literally or too seriously. Emptiness allows you to move on and remain flexible. You can be open to the thoughts and values of others and be ready to change and develop.

You may have to empty yourself of certain parental and family influences that no longer serve you as an adult living your own life. You may have to abandon "truths" that you learned in school or church or from your geographical community. Some regions are notorious for clinging to outdated views and values. Finally, you may have to empty yourself of some of your own long-cherished ideas and opinions, and that process of emptying can be difficult and painful.

We can find so much liberation in our daily lives by including emptiness in everything we do that I consider it the primary doorway to meaning. Modern culture generally doesn't understand the role of emptiness in life, and so we may have to resist pressures around us to frantically fill every minute with activities or explanations or purpose. Therefore, first you resist any temptation to be hyperactive, and then you enjoy calm that comes from letting things take their course.

The Missing Ring

Nasrudin was a spiritual leader and teacher in a small village. He was honored and respected as a mullah, although he was rather unusual and unpredictable.

One day a man of great virtue in the village came to Nasrudin with some news. "My business requires that I move to a town far away, and I regret that I have to leave our beautiful village and the benefits of having you as a spiritual guide and teacher," he said to Nasrudin.

The honored teacher looked sad and said, "I'm very sorry to see you go. I hope you can stay in touch with us, with me."

"I don't know what it will mean to live far away," the man said. "But I had an idea. I have long admired the beautiful ring you wear on the finger of your right hand, and I thought, if you were to give me that ring, every time I looked at my hand and saw that ring I'd think of you."

Now, Nasrudin had his virtues and his ordinary vices. One thing he did not like to do is to part with things that were precious to him.

"I have a better idea," he said. "Why don't I keep my ring.

Then, every day you look at your hand and see that my ring is not there, you will think of me."

⮞⮜

This is a perfect story of emptiness. Instead of seeing something, you see nothing, and that nothing is meaningful. The townsman's attitude is standard: He is about to lose touch with this teacher, so he looks for something. This is how we deal with change and loss. We look for something, anything, to fill the gap.

But Nasrudin is wiser than he looks. He demonstrates the importance of wit and humor in paradoxical teachings. He comes up with a better idea, seeing value in the potential for emptiness he notices in his neighbor. He also perceives that by introducing nothingness in a positive way, he advances the teacher-student relationship. The empty, ringless, unnoticeable finger is the perfect solution.

This leads to broader questions: What place does emptiness have in our relationships? Is it better sometimes not to have physical signs of closeness and love? Is it good to doubt your beloved's devotion to you? Do the things we use to express our love get in the way? You give an expensive gift on an anniversary or on Valentine's Day. Would it be better to find a nongift, an empty gift, one that doesn't cost much or doesn't cost anything, that is not traditional, that has no obvious message?

One of the most satisfying gifts I ever gave my family for Valentine's Day was a little booklet I made myself, translations of a few of Rainer Maria Rilke's poems with brief commentaries. It cost almost nothing. It was useless. Few would appreciate its value, except my family and a few friends. It was utterly simple. I made five copies. I had no commercial intent. The project was riddled with emptiness, but it was satisfying! It was so empty that I have never forgotten it or gotten over the pleasure of giving it.

I try to live by Nasrudin's rule: Do not give away the ring on your finger. Let the other person find meaning in the emptiness that comes from you not giving too much and keeping what is important to you. Giving can be outwardly generous and inwardly selfish. You can get great emotional rewards from giving away too much, but in the end the hidden egotism may ruin the friendship.

This is only one explanation for this particular kind of emptiness, and I am sure there are many others. In true emptiness you don't need or want explanations. As we will see again and again, emptiness itself must be kept empty.

Make it a general rule: Appreciate emptiness wherever you find it. A friend doesn't show up for a dinner date at a restaurant. You sit there looking at the empty chair. Turn your frustration into a meditation on emptiness. Watch what happens when you embrace the empty chair instead of cursing it. Daily you will find yourself faced with limitless presentations of emptiness. First, allow the emptiness by resisting temptations to fill it in. Second, contemplate the new kind of emptiness that has appeared and take lessons from it. Let it stir your imagination so that you can find deeper and richer emptiness in all aspects of your life.

THE LOST ARROW

Harakura was the leading teacher of archery in Japan and drew many students from all over the country and even from other faraway places. His skill with a bow and arrow was renowned, and anyone who wanted to learn these skills came to study with him.

One afternoon after a long three-hour class, Harakura was packing up his equipment when a new student came to him. "Master," he said, "I was very impressed with your skills and your teaching today, and I wonder if you know of the archery master who lives at the top of Mount Kahajaru?"

"No, I haven't heard of him," said the teacher, intrigued.

"I have heard that he is the best archer in the world," the student said. "I think it would be good if you would take the class to the top of this mountain to behold the skills of this most accomplished archer."

"Certainly," said Harakura. "A splendid idea. I will make contact, and perhaps we could make the trip next week."

So the next week Harakura gathered his students around him to prepare them for their journey. "I would think," he said, "that if there were a highly skilled archer in our vicinity, I would have heard of him. But I am willing, of course, to take this class to the top of the mountain in search of a master archer. If you are unimpressed, as I expect will be the case, please be kind to the teacher and certainly to any students he may be training."

So the group set out excitedly for the mountain and the improbable discovery of a teacher who might be better than their own revered Harakura.

They arrived at the foot of the mountain, which reached high into the sky, its top beyond the clouds that day. When they got near the peak of the mountain, they heard some talking and came upon an old man teaching a group of five or six students. He had a beautiful carved wood bow in his hands and was leaning back, aiming at a spot obviously far away up in the sky. The odd thing was that he had no arrow but only the bow. Harakura was about to ask about the missing arrow when the teacher told his students to be very quiet. He pointed to a large bird flying high overhead. Then he pulled back on the bow with all his strength, straining his right arm so that everyone could see the veins poking through under the skin. Of course, there was nothing to pull back — no arrow but only straining fingers on a taut string. Suddenly, he let loose his finger and a moment later the bird fell from the sky. Everyone, including Harakura, was astonished at his skill and asked the old man if they could study with him.

This tale of the empty bowstring is about a special kind of weapon and suggests how to exercise power and be effective in the world.

Sometimes, for example, it is best to keep quiet instead of speaking. Someone criticizes you and expects a defensive response, but you don't say anything. You are not being passive and weak, because it takes considerable strength and special skill to be quiet. Let's call it "the art of holding your tongue" or "the art of not being lured into action" or "the art of using powerful but invisible weapons."

Many people speak too often and say too much. They may say things that are hurtful, when they ought to have kept quiet. This art of not speaking is a good one to master. As a therapist, I make it part of my method. I have trained myself not to speak even when the situation begs for more words.

I am tempted sometimes to offer some advice, to talk about myself, or to explain a situation. But I know that these actions usually don't help much, if at all. It is better sometimes to offer the client a chance to reflect and also to learn from me that speaking is not as important as people think. Not speaking may be just what is needed. Words not heard often hit the target.

In the art of deep conversation, learning how to stay silent is another useful skill. You may feel some tension and be tempted to fill the empty gap with words, any words. Ask yourself, *Do I have the strength to stay quiet?* You may discover that an empty space in a conversation accomplishes more than many words.

In a more general way you may learn how not to do so much or to use your tools with finesse. It may be more effective to use fewer words in an email or letter, or to not write at all. You may not need all the various methods you have at your disposal for communicating.

As a writer, I know that one of the best things I can do to improve a book manuscript is to go through it and cut all unnecessary words. I'm usually shocked at how much that simple exercise does to shorten the book and make the writing clearer. Emptying can be a valuable strategy in many kinds of work. You use nothing to achieve excellent results.

Not doing anything, not explaining yourself, not defending, not showing any external sign of your inward feeling — these are all ways of shooting a bow without an arrow and of honoring holy emptiness. You can get to a point where you appreciate absence over presence and silence over a need to speak. You may have no "weapons" and draw great power from that emptiness. You may become known as a person with odd invisible skills.

You can also lead without any signs of leadership, teach by helping students learn on their own, be a businessperson without making money your main objective. Emptiness abounds, and it promotes life.

Doors and Windows

A wheel's hub may have thirty spokes
but it is the hole in the center that makes it go.
Work clay into a pot
and it is the emptiness in it that makes it useful.
Cut out doors and windows for a room
and these holes make the room livable.
You get something from what is present
but you really benefit from what is absent.
Tao Te Ching

For many years I have kept this teaching from the Tao Te Ching in the forefront of my mind. To me, it is one of the most compelling images for emptiness. Windows in a house make it beautiful and livable, certainly as much as walls and floors. And what would a house be without the empty space of open doors?

I'm inspired to allow empty spaces all over my life: times for doing nothing, gaps in a day's schedule, not going to a place where I'm asked or encouraged to go, saying no to the offer of a job. These are the windows and doorways of my life. Because of those empty passageways I may see things otherwise hidden or visit places otherwise inaccessible.

If you fill up your life, nothing unexpected can happen. You can't make fresh discoveries, and you will have few surprises and revelations.

If you fill up your schedule, then when a profitable opportunity comes along, you will have to say no. If you leave nothing to chance, there will be no unexpected opportunities. If your mind is closed as to what is valuable, you will not learn how to make your life richer and more complex.

Some people assume that life isn't giving them new chances for enrichment, when in fact their doors are closed or even sealed up. Maybe they forgot to put doors into the structure of their lives. Some people's lives are so closed off by the prejudices of their families, church, or society that they can't respond freely or come up with new ideas. In fact, they have no windows in the house of self that might allow them to see the world outside and glimpse new possibilities.

You have to plan and build empty spaces ahead of time so that when an opportunity comes, you can see it and move freely. If you are full of windows and doors there will be many new experiences in your life. You will have enriching events. People will come in and out, and fresh ideas will come and go.

You have emotional spaces that need light, air, and spontaneous visits with friends. Maybe you close up your psychic space out of fear or maybe because you have never considered the importance of doors and windows in your life. That space in your schedule may not be a gap waiting to be filled, but rather a window or a door that is best left open.

Several people have told me of dreams in which a door is ajar or a window open a crack. They are afraid that some evil person might break in. But I feel that the dreamer is often wrong. Their fear may be slightly paranoid. Maybe they need someone to break into their space and usher in new life. Maybe the open window and the door ajar are a grace, and not a threat.

THE EMPTY PLATE

Nasrudin was having dinner with a group of friends at the home of a wealthy and powerful civic leader. The host was obviously competing for attention and watched Nasrudin closely. The servers brought a platter of large, juicy melons for dessert, and the two prominent men ate theirs with gusto.

But then the envious host took his plate of melon rinds and, when Nasrudin wasn't looking, piled them on Nasrudin's plate. "You're a glutton," he said to Nasrudin. "Look at all the melons you ate."

But Nasrudin pointed to his host's empty plate and said, "Well, at least I didn't eat the rinds."

The empty plate in this story tells a whole saga about envy and malice. Nasrudin is able to "read" it and understand that his host's trickery was aimed at diminishing his, Nasrudin's, reputation. The empty plate here does not signify spiritual emptiness but its opposite, plain nothing-ness, the host's trickery and guile. The host would benefit from real emptiness, but instead he neurotically empties his plate to make Nasrudin look bad. The deceitful gesture is the negative, miserly form of the emptiness he lacks.

Pseudo-emptiness abounds in the world. People pre-tend to be selfless while they are secretly serving them-selves. Companies brag about how much money they spend on charity, not mentioning the rewards in taxes they also get or how much greater their profits are than their charitable donations. Advertising makes superlative claims for products, but everyone knows they are exag-gerated at best. Our commercial world would mature and even thrive if it would empty itself of its camouflaged self-interest. It would only help business at a deep level to clear out the widespread manipulations, because, in the end, honesty succeeds.

Of course, we cannot be too pure about this complaint. Advertising and presentation of merchandise require imagi-nation and a degree of excess. Their purpose is to sell you goods. The line between persuasion and manipulation is thin and is often crossed, beyond what is ethical and decent. I am not suggesting perfection but only a move-ment toward holy emptiness.

Pseudo-emptiness may appear as selflessness and generosity. You empty yourself on behalf of another and pretend to be generous when you are not generous at all.

A person may think they are selfless, but they are deluded. Their behavior and motives do not match their ideals.

You may strive to be generous and open to other people's success, but still you may feel a pang of envy. That slight ache is an indication that you have a ways to go in emptying the self. You don't have what your friend has, so you are empty in a sense, but that emptiness is like Nasrudin's host trying to fool everyone with his empty plate. It's not really empty and Nasrudin's is not really full. The feeling of emptiness can be an illusion. You have to probe beneath the surface.

In the tale of the melons, Nasrudin doesn't play the victim, and he playfully exposes the illusion. He is clever in twisting the other man's ploy to unravel the scene. He demonstrates that in matters of ethics and spiritual virtues it may be important to exercise wit and imagination. The ancient Greeks would call this the Hermes spirit, which can be especially important when a heavy dose of virtuousness is in the air. You call out the false piety and use your wit to expose extremes of spiritual posturing, but you don't moralize.

The host's plate is disgusting, Nasrudin's simple and plain, empty in spite of how it looks.

THE LEAKY SACK

The kingdom is like a woman who was carrying a sack full of grain. While she was walking along a road far from home, the bottom of the sack developed a hole, and the grain poured out behind her onto the road. She did not notice what had happened, and when she got home, she put the sack down and discovered that it was empty.

GOSPEL OF THOMAS

This beautiful little story from one of the earliest Gospels tells in parable form what the realm of heaven, the new way of life Jesus teaches, is like. It isn't full of power and authority and riches; it's like a sack with a hole in it that has been emptied out over a long journey. The ideal Jesus describes in this story is not a wealthy, highly structured world religion but a tiny shift in imagination that could transform the planet. Nothing in itself, it gives everything its perfection.

When you think of the simple opening words of this tale, "The kingdom is like…," the story is shocking. You might expect the kingdom to be a place of fruit-laden trees and peaceful animals and virtuous human beings. But here it's a woman carrying a precious sack of nourishing grain, torn and emptied. To find this desired kingdom, you lose things that are precious to you. Even treasured beliefs must be emptied if you want to live in a community dedicated to love.

Jesus offers other images of emptying: "the first shall be last," "sell what you have and give it to the poor," "he who has nothing will lose what he has." This is an essential lesson for all leaders, but especially spiritual teachers and community organizers. You can only do your job when you are the servant, when you are the least of the members, when you never forget that you are also a follower. At any moment when you feel you are above the person next to you, you could remember the woman standing in her home with her empty sack. She doesn't have the grain she expected, but she has the secret to a loving world. She knows that whatever she does has to be emptied of self-absorption.

A good leader identifies with their subjects and students and resists the temptation to pursue ego satisfactions. They especially don't make up for their own lack of self-worth by exploiting their leadership role for personal emotional gain. Nothing could be more obscene and contradictory than reports of honored spiritual teachers taking sexual advantage of their students. But there are more subtle ways to lord it over your followers and feed your own superiority.

The stories Jesus tells and those told about him often contain potent images of emptiness. The story of the loaves of bread and pieces of fish is also a metaphor. When you have nothing but a few scraps, then you will be supremely and miraculously nourished. When your fishing boat is empty and you have been fishing all night, simply put your net on the other side, and it will suddenly be full. Emptiness and fullness are surprisingly close to each other. They are on either side of your boat. If you want to be full, you have to start with emptiness.

A key word describes the role of Jesus as a model for the perfected human being: *kenosis*, or "emptying." He emptied himself to be completely receptive to his Father's plans. We can empty in that sense, as well, allowing life to shape us and make us into who we deeply want to be. In a state of kenosis, you don't need to plan and control everything, but you allow constant change and transformation. You can empty yourself of your plans and agendas and in that way be open to the Father's wishes and accept the design that life itself has for you. The Father is the Logos aspect of life, its universal order and your role in the greater design.

Imagine you were going to tell someone about your

vision for a future, a utopia, a grand experiment in the best of humanity, and you said you imagined it like a leaky sack. Imagine a world leader emptying himself so he could have the welfare of his people in mind. Imagine a parent being so empty that she could help her child find his destiny and not just do what she wants. Imagine lovers emptying themselves so they could think always of the relationship instead of their own needs.

This story tells of a self-emptying over time, not intentionally, but by accident or fate. The ancient Greeks might say that this emptying is the work of Hermes the Thief, the life principle that steals from us for our own good. We might lose our health, an important relationship, some cherished object, a planned project. Most of us are forever losing something precious to us. Every day, it seems, we are emptied of something, as kenosis rules our lives.

The woman in the story lost what she toiled to get and what she hoped she would have in her home. You can imagine her thoughts and feelings on discovering the leak in her sack. Have you ever had something that was precious to you suddenly start leaking? A job that no longer fulfills, a relationship that no longer brings joy, a talent that isn't as remarkable as it once was, success that slowly turns to failure. This kind of emptying may lead you to discover deeper love, greater empathy toward others, or a more giving and worthwhile way of being in society. When you sense the leak in what you hold precious, know that the great kingdom of the sky is nearby.

We might also notice that it is when the woman gets home from the marketplace that she discovers that her precious cargo was emptied. When we are out doing too much, our thoughts too complicated and our goals vast and full of self-regard, we need to go home to our most private and comfortable place and discover again how some things we cherish are emptying out. In the thick of an active life it may be impossible to notice what has become empty. Back home, in the quiet of an evening, we may sit back and reflect and in that silent moment discover the joy of emptiness.

A Quiet Night

A quiet night behind my grass hut.
Alone, I play a stringless lute.
Its melody drifts to the wind-blown clouds and fades.
Its sound deepens with the running stream,
expanding till it fills a deep ravine,
and echoes through the vast woods.
Who, other than a deaf person,
can hear this faint song?
RYOKAN

I became a musician one day in about my seventh year when I was visiting friends with my parents. My father showed me the piano our friends had and invited me to play a few notes. I was hooked. Later he bought an old upright piano for our house and wrote the notes of the scale on the keys in pencil and taught me how to move my fingers to play a scale. After I had some lessons, he pulled out his violin and we played duets together. My father was a good musician and could play difficult pieces, and one day he called out from another room to tell me one of the piano keys was out of tune: it wasn't playing F. I discovered that my father had perfect pitch.

At age thirteen I left home and lived in a monastery for over a dozen years. There I conducted Gregorian chant, which is music intended to nurture monastic quiet and to calm the heart and ease the yearning spirit. I found that some music can quiet you down and lead you to a silence of the soul.

So I appreciate this poem by Ryokan about a stringless lute that fills the hills and hollows of the natural world and can be heard only by a deaf person. How do you play a lute that doesn't have any strings? With great subtlety. I imagine playing my piano for deaf people, enjoying the flow of sounds and silences between us.

Quiet is a form of emptiness and is important for people who need to reflect and remember. Learning how to live a quiet life is an important art, especially in a world that carelessly assaults us with noise. How can you know yourself if you can't hear your thoughts or the beating of your heart?

You don't have to aim for absolute silence. Quiet is even better. Cultivating a contemplative quality of life helps you be less excitable when events come at you with a fever. Quiet gives you equilibrium and an environment in which you can see what is happening and make good decisions. Quiet prepares you for the sounds of activity.

Now picture a person playing a lute or guitar that has no strings. As an image, what would it imply? Music to be felt with an interior ear, a mystical kind of music. Maybe the strings are there but not heard. Music for the subtle body. Music that is not so literal as to be perceived by sense organs but some other kind of organ. When you behold Picasso's blue painting of a guitar player, do you imagine music coming out of it? When you recite Wallace Stevens's "The Man with the Blue Guitar," do you understand that music is much broader in meaning than the sounds we hear from instruments? Does life have rhythm, melody, harmony?

There is a profound paradox in this poem about the lute without strings: An object made to create harmonious sounds is silent. Maybe silence is the sound we are looking for. Maybe music can create the silence we need in order to hear the music of the world.

Is life itself something to be played as if it were a musical instrument, say, a lute? Does it want to be plucked in order to be perceived and enjoyed? Maybe you would have to be deaf to the world's actual sounds in order to hear its deeper music.

For many years now, we have had in our home an almost life-size wood statue made in Indonesia of a temple flute player. He has been playing for our family all this time, as the children have grown up and as the parents have made their artistic contributions to the world. Without being precious about it, you can imagine a silent music filling a home, the flute player offering an important lesson each time a family member notices him.

Now when I go to art museums and see paintings of angels playing their instruments silently, I try to hear their music with my literal ears turned down low. For me, it's a lesson in how subtle life is and how you often have to listen with an inner ear to what is being said in the world. You have to hear the silent sound, the stringless lute, the angel's trumpet, the mute voice that alone can make sounds that penetrate the soul.

Nothing Is Natural

True practice of zazen is to sit as if drinking water when you are thirsty. There you have naturalness. It is quite natural for you to take a nap when you are very sleepy. But to take a nap just because you are lazy, as if it were the privilege of a human being to take a nap, is not naturalness. You think, "My friends, all of them, are napping; why shouldn't I? ..." This is not naturalness. Your mind is entangled with some other idea, someone else's idea, and you are not independent, not yourself, and not natural.... True being comes out of nothingness, moment after moment. Nothingness is always there, and from it everything appears.
    SHUNRYU SUZUKI

≈

At the heart of the beautiful teachings of Zen master Shunryu Suzuki is this lesson on emptiness as naturalness and nothingness. Here, it is a quality of life: to drink when you are thirsty and take a nap when you are tired.

Do everything, he says, in that spirit. Don't fill your mind with annoying inner discussions about being a good person or letting other people see how advanced you are. He says later that even Zen practice that looks good from the outside can be unnatural because of your interfering thoughts and motives. It's takes work, he says, to reach that level of naturalness.

A person who is forever scheming inside their head appears neurotic. You notice that their bodily presence and facial expressions are too complicated. There is too much going on. Too many layers of intentionality. You cannot really trust a person who is unnatural, because you don't know who the real person is or what they have in mind.

Your thoughts and actions have to arise from nothingness, from an empty place that is not full of unnecessary plots and motives. You drink water because you are thirsty, not because you want to show everyone that you are an exceptional person thanks to your healthy habits. That is neurotic, not natural. It has none of the emptiness that allows an action to be natural.

You may think that you could never arrive at such an advanced degree of naturalness, to be entirely free of neurosis. But you can move in that direction, and at each step you will be freer and more joyous. People will relate to you, perhaps, with less of their own neurotic habits. Your interactions will not be perfect, but they will be cleaner. The flow between you and someone else will be easier.

When your actions and presence arise out of nothingness, when they are empty, both you and others know who you are. They are free to relate to you in their own way without being manipulated into a certain kind of response. Imagine how this kind of naturalness could help a marriage or other intimate relationship. It could be the panacea for marital discord and maybe even world conflicts.

Picture the empty marriage, in the sense we are taking the word *empty*. It would be free of paranoid thoughts, such as assuming that the other person is doing bad things to you and trying to make life difficult. Your expectations would be lighter, less demanding, and more flexible.

Imagine emptiness in advertising. You could trust it to tell you exactly what is good about a product and not to trick you into paying for something that you don't need or that doesn't work. Modern life is dangerously lacking in emptiness and naturalness. Politicians have too little of it, and financial managers are often coming up with schemes for pilfering your precious dollars — the very opposite of emptiness.

In spite of the neurotic field all around us, you can aim for emptiness in daily life. You could talk to a friend with all the naturalness of taking a drink of water when you are thirsty. You will realize what is going on in you and simply show it, without the slightest dissembling or manipulation. Maybe you will have images of a flute player or an angel with a graceful viol playing their music silently, reminding you to be quiet, inwardly and out-wardly, as you go about your life.

Living with naturalness is a little different from living naturally. Living naturally, you might want to eat organic foods, spend time in nature, try to avoid the complexities of modern life, live off the grid, and try not to spoil nature with pollution and excessive development. Living with naturalness in Suzuki's definition, you don't let your bothersome selfish motives get in the way, or your fears and anxieties. You deal with them by simply being present to what you are doing and clearing your mind of manipulating and self-conscious thoughts. It can be done.

One of the best ways I know to learn this naturalness is in ordinary conversations with people. If someone asks you, "How are you doing?" you don't have thoughts of trying to impress or get sympathy or control the outcome or establish a good image of yourself. You let these common interferences slide away, and you speak simply and directly. You may also want to avoid the usual clichés that say nothing. "I'm doing well, except that I'm tired from working too much lately and I'm sad about the state of the world." Notice the simple adjectives, *tired* and *sad*, that clearly express your emotions. There is nothing here to complicate them or make them confusing. You're not manipulating your friend, trying to be seen in the way you would like to be seen. You simply express who you are at the moment.

Where is the emptiness here? In the missing manipulations and unnecessary complexities. Your friend can trust what you say because of what is missing from your words: all the guile and control that is so common in our interactions. Your friend can actually sense your emptiness, and it is refreshing and trustworthy.

I had a friend, James Hillman, who I thought was good, at least with me, at expressing himself naturally. One day I asked him the usual simple question: "How are you doing today, Jim?" "I'm as mad as hell," he said. "Why don't people take care of animals instead of treating them like beasts?" Quite clear. Frequently his answer to the question was: "I'm depressed. It takes so much work to get a book out, mine or someone else's." He was a publisher as well as a writer. I never heard him say, "I'm fine. How are you?"

But this is just a start. From here you let your breath flow directly and easily. You don't hold back and make things complicated. Your sentences are not felt on many levels. Only one. You say what you feel and what you mean. The rest is empty.

The Cucumber Sandwiches

ALGERNON: *Have you got the cucumber sandwiches cut for Lady Bracknell?*

LANE [manservant]: *Yes, sir.* [Hands them on a salver.] ...

[JACK puts out his hand to take a sandwich. Algernon at once interferes.]

ALGERNON: *Please don't touch the cucumber sandwiches. They are ordered specially for Aunt Augusta.* [Takes one and eats it.]

JACK: *Well, you have been eating them all the time.*

ALGERNON: *That is quite a different matter. She is my aunt....*

[Enter LADY BRACKNELL.]

LADY BRACKNELL: *And now I'll have a cup of tea, and one of those nice cucumber sandwiches you promised me....*

ALGERNON: [Picking up empty plate in horror.] *Good heavens! Lane! Why are there no cucumber sandwiches? I ordered them specially.*

LANE: [Gravely] *There were no cucumbers in the market this morning, sir. I went down twice.*
ALGERNON: *No cucumbers!*

OSCAR WILDE

∽

In the opening minutes of Oscar Wilde's play *The Importance of Being Earnest*, the characters Jack (who in the city calls himself Ernest) and Algernon have a food problem. A plate of cucumber sandwiches is ready for Jack's aunt, Lady Bracknell, who is expected soon and hopes to be served her favorite — cucumber sandwiches. But Algernon eats them all, so that when the aunt arrives, the plate is empty.

The simple truth is that the man couldn't resist eating the sandwiches when they were in front of him, but he feigns innocence when his aunt has no cucumber sandwiches to eat. He pretends that he has no idea why the plate is empty. His butler compounds the deception by saying that there were no cucumbers at the market that morning. Oscar Wilde's apparent purpose is to lampoon the morals of high society in his time, to show how morally vacant it was. The fabricated reason for the empty plate shows that there is no natural honesty in the people — plain, worthwhile emptiness — but only vacant avoidance of truth.

What Wilde's society needs is real emptiness, a life

without all the deceptions. Wilde portrays other kinds of manipulation: Algernon uses an imaginary friend who lives in the country, Bunbury, as an excuse whenever he needs one. Algernon's friend Ernest is also a fabrication. In London he goes by the name Ernest and has a shady character, while in the country he is known as Jack and is a perfect gentleman. High and low morals in one character. Such a split requires deep internal subterfuge, and so just about nothing in the man or the entire play has any of the naturalness and guilelessness of spiritual emptiness.

The Jack/Ernest split echoes the split between a person saying what they want to say and clouding it with evasions and complications, as if two persons were speaking. We all have within us, at times, Jack and Ernest. They speak at the same time but with different meanings and concerns.

But we have to remember that Oscar Wilde was a man of wit, deep understanding, high values, and a big heart. For him, the empty plate shows us where thoughtfulness and kindness could be. Algernon could either have left the cucumber sandwiches for the aunt or at least told her the truth about their disappearance.

In his satirical style Wilde dramatizes how society can be full of pretense, when it should be guileless. The characters go through various contortions of language to manipulate the people around them, and these contortions destroy any chance for naturalness.

There is no real emptiness in the simple situations of

this famous play. Instead we find many forms of vacancy, especially a lack of character and morality. I am using the word *vacancy* to describe what happens when genuine emptiness is not to be found. Vacancy — no morals, no character, no honesty — is the symptomatic or neurotic expression of a possible deep-seated emptiness, no guile, no lies, no dissembling. With real emptiness, you may not have any hidden agendas. With pseudo-emptiness you may have self-serving goals that you keep to yourself.

In a way then, *The Importance of Being Earnest*, even the title itself, is a plea for emptiness. If your name is Jack, keep it. Don't use another one someplace else to pretend that you are another kind of person. This attitude fits with Wilde's life philosophy: If you are a thief, be one, and don't pretend you're not.

Wilde's entire play is about the confusion that arises when people are not direct but always playing games with each other. It is astonishing that the world hums along as well as it does, given the false testimonies and prevarications that stuff business, politics, and daily conversation. Plain speaking is a virtue we might pursue for our own benefit and for the future of humanity. It would be liberating to be straightforward, fearless, and, when the occasion requires, earnest.

THERE IS NO DRIVER

*One day the teacher Nasrudin, in London on a visit, hopped on
a double-decker bus and went up to the upper level. He sat for
a few minutes and looked around, then he went back down to
the lower level.*

"What's the problem?" said the ticket collector.

"There is no driver up there," he said.

This does not sound like an authentic Nasrudin story, but
it will do. It is certainly in the spirit of the Sufi stories.

As one who listens to the dreams of others almost
every day, I recognize something familiar in this story.
People all over the world dream about transportation.
Apparently, the psyche is in movement, or often is, or
should be. People dream of cars, trains, buses, and air-
planes — frequently. Sometimes the dreamer is being

driven, but sometimes, rarely, they are in the driver's seat. Sometimes it is a train, more often an airplane. In the latter case, the dreamer may be the pilot or a passenger. I've heard a few dreams about buses, but no double-deckers so far.

It makes a difference whether you are driving or not. Are you in control, or are you letting someone else — some other urge or spirit in you — take over? When someone else is driving, you are willing to be led and may get to your destination safely. If you are driving or piloting, you need the skill to control your vehicle. I like to use the word *vehicle* because in it you can hear the broader concept of having a way to move from one place to another or one state of being to another. Ancient writings on the soul refer to its "vehicle," like Plato's chariot, and Buddhism was called a large or small vehicle — *mahayana* and *hinayana*. Buddhism is also a raft to get you across to the other side, where you can live without suffering.

Sometimes the journey of the dream seems to be about the whole voyage of your life, as you move from one career or relationship or lifestyle to another. Sometimes it is only about a small trip. Whatever size it is, the transportation dream may signal passage to a new stage of your life.

In our story, Nasrudin is not comfortable moving to his next destination without a driver. If this were a dream, I would wonder if the dreamer had trouble trusting something other than their own ability and will to steer their way through life. Sometimes you have to trust the movement and read the signs, letting fate or destiny guide you. The driver's seat in this case may be empty or nonexistent.

Joseph Campbell has a beautiful passage in one of his books on mythology concerning the tale of Tristan and Isolde, where Tristan is in a small boat with no oars or rudder but only a harp, drifting toward the next station in his destiny, Ireland and his love Isolde: "Tristan, resting trustingly on the bosom of those cosmic powers by which the movements of the heavens and all things on earth are controlled, has been carried on the concord of his Orphic-Irish harp, resounding to the music of the sea and spheres, to that very Dublin Bay where Joyce's hero Dedalus was to go walking centuries later, questioning his heart as to whether he would ever have the courage to entrust himself to life."

This long sentence beautifully describes the situation any human being might face as they launch a new career or project, or risk marriage, or move to another part of the world. The theme of trust, faith in yourself and your world, and the willingness to go out on the rough ocean of life without control is a turning point for most people. Usually we aren't given a compass or a rudder.

In a comic way, the story about Nasrudin and the bus pokes fun at our fear of going ahead without a driver, someone in control of our journey. But our Tristan nature is quite the opposite: We can find our way by trusting in life and giving up the need to be in control.

Often it appears that what drives a person's decisions is the ego, but that may be because we in the modern world are not much in tune with other figures, other selves, that have an impact on our emotions and desires. They, too, can drive us to make decisions and move us in certain directions.

What if there is no ego, but only the various persons of the psyche making their wishes felt? Then we may not have an actual driver, like a bus driver at the wheel, but only a slew of passions and fears. What if the one in charge we so depend upon doesn't show up? What if their seat is empty? In particular, what if the "man upstairs" is not in his place, and the upper region has no controller? Then we may be left either to do the driving ourselves or to get along with our intuitions and our faith. Maybe then we will descend, and come down to earth, and learn to trust life to take us where we need to go.

Break the Molecules

God must, in some way or other, make room for himself, hollowing us out and emptying us, if he is finally to penetrate into us. And in order to assimilate us in him, he must break the molecules of our being so as to re-cast and re-model us....It will put us into the state organically needed if the divine fire is to descend upon us.

TEILHARD DE CHARDIN

A Jesuit priest, Pierre Teilhard de Chardin was also a paleontologist who did significant scientific work in China and was involved in the discovery of Peking Man in the 1920s. Through his intense spiritual and scientific practice, he became a visionary philosopher who extended the idea of evolution to include the spiritual transformation of humanity.

Chardin was often in trouble with the Vatican, which

forbade his books to be placed in religious libraries or even in bookshops. He was not even allowed to publish and lecture. Once, he was awarded an honor by Boston College, but while he was on his way to accept the award, it was rescinded. One wonders what was so dangerous or threatening in his thought to warrant such strong repression.

He coined several special terms for his vision, such as *Christogenesis* and *Omega Point*, contemporary life coming to a place where it finally discovers the primacy of unsentimental, honest love. In the above passage he picks up our theme of emptying, indicating that for our spiritual evolution we need to be emptied out so we can be remodeled. The divine will "break the molecules of our being" so that we can be transformed by a mysterious fire.

But what are the molecules of your being, and how can they be broken in a positive way? They're the building blocks of who you are. You can't get much more basic. Not just your emotions or your thoughts, but your identity in the deepest possible way. You could say, your very soul.

All of this has to be broken up so that you can restructure yourself and move into your adulthood. From Chardin's point of view, we don't know who we really are. We are still too young, too immature, and too superficial. We don't take our lives seriously enough because we still don't know the nature of the world into which we were born. We think that our lives center around the physical world: making better machines and discovering the vast reaches of our universe. But eventually we may learn that life is essentially and positively mysterious, not to be explained and exploited but absorbed into us. We may ultimately discover that love is not an emotion but the central dynamic of the world's welfare and existence.

Think of the explorers of the fifteenth and sixteenth centuries. They thought they were making the mind-blowing discovery of a new world. But to us, they were only making a trip to the Caribbean islands on absurdly fragile and handmade crafts. In the not-too-distant future, people will look at our achievements in the same light. To reach Chardin's vision for humanity we would have to advance at a different level. We would not be making progress in the same material projects but crossing a barrier into an altogether new way of envisioning life and the purpose of our lives.

For a long while, the religions and spiritual traditions kept our minds at least partially focused on possibilities beyond the physical, but eventually those traditions eroded and came to serve the materialist viewpoint, or sustained such a division of spirit and matter that we haven't yet learned how to live a meaningful life in a material world. Today, the invisible and the infinite have almost no relation to the material world to which we devote our energies.

So this identity we have and the worldview we are so proud of have to be blasted and opened up. All this pride in our discoveries and inventions has to be drenched in emptiness. We have to become less attached to it and less inflated by it. Both our values and our emotions need emptying. Or so Chardin implies in his passionate cry for change.

Above all, we need a new understanding and appreciation of the divine. We cannot use the word *God* any longer without extensive footnotes quoting Meister Eckhart and Dietrich Bonhoeffer, who remained Christians even as they emptied the very notion of God. This is not in any way atheistic or secularistic. It is a renewal of religion. No, we can hardly use the word *religion*, either, any longer without pause. Like *God*, it has been rigidified and sentimentalized, thereby losing its force and meaning. We have to find alternative ways to keep our vision infinite and mysterious. Spirituality itself needs to be emptied, and Chardin coined new words to picture humanity evolving in its purpose. He demonstrated that we need a new language for spiritual matters, words that inspire us toward a new way of being.

THE WINE RAN OUT

On the third day there was a wedding in Cana of Galilee, and Jesus's mother was there, and both Jesus and his students had been invited. The wine ran out and Jesus's mother said to him, "They don't have any more wine."

Jesus said to her, "Dear woman, what does that have to do with you and me? My time has not yet come."

His mother told the waiters, "Do whatever he tells you."

There were six stone water jars set out for the Jewish ritual of purification. Each could hold twenty or thirty gallons. Jesus told them, "Fill the jars with water." So they filled them up to the brim. Then he said, "Pour some out now and take it to the wedding planner." So they took it to him.

When the wedding planner had tasted the water that had become wine, he called the groom. He didn't know where the wine had come from, though the waiters knew because they had poured it out. He told the groom, "Most people serve the good wine first, and then when people have had a lot to drink, *they serve the less expensive varieties. But you kept the excellent wine until now."*

GOSPEL OF JOHN

꩜

This beautiful, well-known story from the Gospel of John compresses the entire Jesus philosophy into a single image: the shift from water to wine. When you adopt the Jesus way, you go from a rule-based, guilt-ridden life (purifying water) to a life of joy and pleasure (inebriating wine). The jars in which the miraculous wine appeared were meant to hold water for ritual cleansing. When a guest arrived, he could wash his hands ritually, signifying the purity of his intentions. Jesus replaces concern about purity with wine's intoxication, joy, and celebration. When you look closely at the Gospel stories, you find many scenes of parties and convivial dinners, which are not entirely literal but portray a philosophy of love and holy pleasure.

Has society today "run out of wine"? Have we become too preoccupied with work and making money and being busy? Has our capacity for celebration diminished? Our parties often seem to be a compensation for working hard or trying to follow the rules. As a therapist, I often find that people feel so much guilt from their past that they can't enjoy life. Or they feel obligated to spend their time working too hard. So their partying becomes compulsive, and as such it is not deeply satisfying and meaningful. It has to be emptied so the Dionysian may enter, giving our celebrations meaning.

The Greeks associated wine with the god Dionysus, who was one of the resurrected deities, a god of life and death. He represented intense vitality and a rhythm of dying and rising. Throughout history artists and theologians have seen a Dionysian strain in Jesus. He died and resurrected, he compared his blood to wine, and there is the tantalizing story of his wine-making abilities. Our celebrations and parties could become truly Dionysian in spirit, unleashing a full-bodied joy in living. There could be less actual drinking and more celebrating in the spirit of Dionysus. Perhaps it could be said that the more alcohol is consumed at a party, the less Dionysus is present.

Just as Dionysus is dismembered and resurrects, and the grape is crushed and returns as wine, so a person might be emptied to discover a new kind of life. Marriage is a dying to an old life and a rising to a new kind of experience. The main teaching of Jesus is to die to the old, legalistic way of making sense of your life and rise to a more joyful philosophy based on the principle of love.

In the story of the wedding in Cana, we are first faced with the empty jars. Then with no gesture, no abracadabra, no lifting of a veil, Jesus produces a miraculous transformation: Jars once empty, then filled with water, now hold excellent wine. Jesus brings profound joy and celebration to marriage and human intimacy.

Note also the presence of Jesus's mother and her role

in the event's unfolding. She sees that the wine has run out, a slight indication that she, too, venerated for centuries, has a Dionysian spirit. She represents the maternal aspect of Jesus's teaching and example. She supports his philosophy, one that is unlike the mainly male, abstract, and demanding schools of philosophers and religious organizations. His way is caring, and it shows a profound appreciation for basic human needs. Mary is genuinely concerned about the party running out of wine. In a bigger sense, she is aware that the Dionysian is being lost.

If you adopt Jesus's teaching, what happens to you? This parable tells us that you shift from being a moralist to being an epicurean, a lover of life's deep and simple pleasures. Jesus attends dinner parties and encourages one woman to rub oil on his feet. In one of the alternative Gospels, Jesus leads his friends in a dance. This is not an austere approach to a meaningful life, but one that appreciates pleasure and encourages joy, not superficial entertainment but the joy that comes from being in tune with the laws of life, what in India they call *ananda*.

In the Upanishads we find that rich spirituality summarized in a term composed of three words: *sat-cit-ananda*: being, awareness, and joy. *Ananda* is the deep joy of being true to your nature and to the ways of life. This is the joy that Jesus teaches, and he embodies it in the happiness of being with his friends and family members, in good dinners, and in making fine wine for a wedding celebration.

Today we are in desperate need of this joy. We believe in cool virtue and have forgotten the importance of warm friendship and felt community. We focus on rules and personal success, finding less and less time for celebration and fun and intimate gathering. We are often like clean, empty jars, waiting to become vessels of intoxicating joy. But from a positive point of view, our very emptiness is preparation for a remarkable resurgence of a joyful spiritual life: the Dionysian Jesus.

The Empty Carriage

Rabbi Elimelech of Lizhensk is sitting in his carriage one day as his driver takes him toward his destination. A group of people see him in the carriage and start following him in the street, and the crowd gets bigger and bigger. The rabbi hears the sound of the band of people following him, so he asks the driver, "What is all the commotion about?"

The driver says, "The people want to follow holiness and virtue."

"Oh," says the rabbi, "so do I." So he gets out and joins the crowd following the now empty carriage.

❧

It is quite natural for a spiritual teacher to feel superior and to expect deference. Knowledge, skill, experience, standing, credentials, titles — they can all go to your head and make you think that you are special. How many leaders could step out of the carriage, ignore their petty ego strokes, and follow wisdom? Many spiritual leaders do not understand the paradox whereby the best leader is a good follower, the best teacher a good student. When you teach, you keep in mind that you love learning. When you study, you remember that you follow your teacher but always learn from yourself. The paradigm of teacher and student should never be split into two separate people. The two of you together follow the empty carriage of wisdom.

The emptiness of learning means that you, the teacher, full of information and skills, are not the focus of your students. They need to follow wisdom and holiness, for knowledge is one of the holiest things in the world. It makes life worthwhile. The teacher points toward knowledge and is not the origin of knowledge.

You also have to realize that you, too, are seeking an invisible goal that is empty, not personal success but maybe the advancement of humanity through education. Your pet theories and practices cannot be so set and fixed that they become rigid. You have to tend their emptiness, and that is a difficult task. Imagine a Jungian psychologist saying, "Jung doesn't have all the answers," or a scientist admitting, "There is a lot to learn beyond science."

When your students and followers show their love for you, don't take it so personally. They are charmed by the vision you have given them and an approach to learning that makes their lives substantial and meaningful. You are the conduit, not the true object of attention. When you hear the clamor of approval, know that this is a signal to get out of your honorable carriage and join with your students in honoring the invisible values that are so precious.

WE ARE LEFT AS TRACES

We are left as traces, lasting in our very thinness like the scarcely visible lines on a Chinese silkscreen, microlayers of pigment and carbon, which can yet portray the substantial profundities of a face. Lasting no longer than a little melody, a unique composition of disharmonious notes, yet echoing long after we are gone. This is the thinness of our aesthetic reality, this old, very dear image that is left and lasts.

JAMES HILLMAN

These are the last lines of James Hillman's book *The Force of Character*, and they are the words I recited at his funeral while standing at his graveside. James left us a perfect description of the frailty and beauty of a human life. In the scope of things it is not much, but nevertheless it is lasting and melodious.

Let me say a word about James and the emptiness he

describes. In his youth he wandered the world and studied at major educational meccas such as the Sorbonne and Trinity College in Dublin. He discovered Jung and became an expert on Jung's thinking. But he also developed his own psychology, departing from Jung's exact teachings where he thought it was appropriate. He was reviled and criticized bitterly by fellow scholars, and yet he kept his sights on his own guidance; inspired by Jung's example, he stayed loyal to the vision he found in himself.

He followed his daimon, a guiding voice or urge, and knew the beauty and pain of heeding his inner guidance. He was a powerful teacher because he allowed these voices to speak through him. He honored his teachers from the past and never suffered fools. That is, he never joined up with the latest bubble of pseudo-wisdom appearing on the scene. He went his own way and created a body of work that I believe will stand with the wisdom of the ages.

This approach to learning and teaching is an example of profound emptiness. You have to be empty to allow the genius to enter and shape you. To be an effective creator you have to step aside and let your ancestors use you to complete their efforts of ages past. For we end these gossamer lives incomplete, in a way, turning over the precious matters we toiled at to those coming after us. We leave with a significant and useful degree of emptiness. Our legacy to the future is not only what we accomplished but what we left unfinished.

James's words teach us that emptiness itself is not always absolute. We notice it in the small pieces left behind, the leak in the sack, the tiny amount of fish and bread we have to feed thousands. Emptiness itself must be empty, or else it can't empty us.

As I write this, I am eighty years old. Like my friend Hillman, I hope to leave traces of my reflections on human life in a slew of books and in the passing thoughts of students and friends. In my view, we are drifting, smoky shapes that add the tiniest element to human perfection. Yet those microscopic additions are of the greatest value in moving humanity along the path of its maturing. Small is beautiful and tiny is precious.

WHERE DOES MY LAP GO?

The anxiety-laden problem of what will happen to me when I die is, after all, like asking what happens to my fist when I open my hand, or where my lap goes when I stand up.
    ALAN WATTS

~~

The greatest emptiness of all is the space left when we pass on. When I read Alan Watts's witty image of a fist opening or a lap disappearing, I think of the movement of a magician. There is something magical about appearing in this world and then disappearing. It's like a magician making a card or a coin appear and disappear. At birth we suddenly find ourselves in this world, in our time, with our passionate concerns. Then suddenly we are not here, and we don't know where we go.

We may have beliefs, suppositions, and hints about

the disappearing act of death, but no one knows for certain how it all works, if it works at all. Whatever happens, life is incredibly short, and, especially as you get older, you keep thinking of the end. It would help to have a positive and uplifting idea of this ending, but you don't want an illusion just to make you feel better.

My own way of dealing with this important matter is to try to think it through carefully. I don't want to delude myself or just find an escape from it by choosing one of the beliefs at hand: heaven, reincarnation, nothing. I appreciate the many variations on these solutions, and I can accept them all to a point. But more convincing to me is to understand that science doesn't know everything. I suspect that the world is far more mysterious than the one science tolerates. There are many mysteries and puzzles, many unexplained phenomena. Besides, I don't believe that I am the brain-directed entity of modern laboratory psychology. I live a meaningful life with deep thoughts and deep emotions. I have hopes and fears for my generation, and these experiences do not come from a purely physical being. In other words, I sense that I and my fellow humans have a soul. Jung said that this soul is not fully dependent on the body, and I sense that in myself. So the vision I have of human life is not just physical and gives me hope about my last disappearing trick.

I was raised a Catholic with a belief in eternal life. I may have grown out of many of the childish beliefs I was taught, but as an adult I can reframe those beliefs and honor them. I don't need to outsmart my parents and teachers by rejecting their beliefs altogether.

The final factor that gives me hope in the face of the apparent emptiness that bookends my life is the love I feel for those who have been and are close to me. Love feels timeless and is not just physical. It would have to be a cynical universe to shut down such intense love in mid-course, and I can't live with that degree of cynicism.

It helps me to think of my life not as a long narrative of separate events following one another on a straight, extending line. For me, time is not unfolding but an instant in the immeasurable present. The events of my life appear one by one to create a circle of anecdotes around me. They all exist in a moment, and at every instant I am the collection of those events plus the one happening in this instant.

I cultivate a virtue, a power of heart, that I learned as a young person — hope. This is not the expectation that something I want will be given to me. It is an open-ended trust in life, a trust that is not naive. I know what hope feels like, even when there is no specific expectation. This is the hope you tap into when a doctor tells you that the medical world can't do anything for you. The hope you can reach for then is not reasonable and has little to do with evidence. It is a power of soul that sustains you in the presence of mystery and despair.

I like Alan Watts's images for the final disappearance in part because they are fun and simple. I suspect that the joy coming out of hope can make death at least tolerable, and the simplicity of standing up shows how much a part of death it can be. It is so simple that any effort we make could be unnoticeable.

NOTHING MORE

Early in the morning on the first day of the week, the women went to the tomb with the spices they had prepared but discovered that the stone had been rolled away from the tomb. When they entered, they didn't see the body of the master....Then they left the tomb and reported everything to the Eleven, and others, too. These women included Mary of Magdala, Joanna, and Mary the mother of James....So Peter left and ran to the tomb. He bent over and looked and saw the linen wrappings. Nothing more.

GOSPEL OF LUKE

This Gospel tells one of the greatest emptiness stories in all of history: Jesus's empty tomb. Try to picture the events of the story: for a long time Jesus had been giving hints that he would rise on the third day. Now it's three days since the execution, and a group of his women followers go to the tomb where they know he was buried, and they see the linen wrappings, but no Jesus. No body. The tomb is empty. Linen fabric and, in the Greek, *mona*. Nothing more. That's all!

This empty tomb is the most important and most extraordinary of all details about Jesus in the Gospels. He is not there. That means he has resurrected. And *resurrected* means "gone." Where he was in this life is now empty. Resurrection then becomes the most important theme in the life of Jesus. The empty tomb is his essence. He had told his followers that they would now embody his presence by living his values.

But what does it mean? Is the story of resurrection really history? Did Jesus actually resurrect, literally and physically? Many think this way. Or is it a story about the reality of Jesus's teachings? Are we all supposed to rise up out of our ignorant and ineffective lives? Is the empty tomb a sign that our dormancy is over? We are now awake. We know infinitely better what life is all about and how to continue.

The image of the empty tomb is a stark wake-up call: You can get up from the deadening life you lead, and resurrect. Live the new resurrected life of the kingdom that Jesus preached. The Buddha, of course, had a similar awakening experience. He left the protections of his family home and beheld age, illness, death, and the monk's life, and he woke up. He is known as "the Awakened One."

The Greek word used in the Gospels, *egeiro*, can mean either "rise" or "wake up."

How are we dormant? Primarily by being absorbed into cultural ways of thinking and finding meaning. We accept what we are offered by the media as important values, and we don't question them. We also sleep in the habits of our families, usually generations of them. We absorb their blindness and unthinking ways. We sleep in traditional religion by accepting childish beliefs and superficial values.

It is never enough to accept and absorb any teaching. You have to consider it carefully, let it unfold, mature, and become, at least in part, your own. It has to live in you and not lie like a corpse in the center of your mind. If you allow it to be lifeless, you will sleep your life away.

You are asleep when you get a job or choose a career merely for income and give up your attention to a life work that constantly shifts and develops. Up until the end you have to be open to change and unexpected turns. You can't get too comfortable because that is the position for sleeping, not working.

If people look into the mausoleum of your self at the end of a marriage or career or another important chapter in your life, they should see that it is empty. You have resurrected. You are not a decomposing body of a self, but newly alive and at work. The old self is no longer present.

You have gone on. You woke up frequently over the course of your life and left your tomb empty.

The empty tomb of the Gospels is a sign that, whatever death you have gone through, you can resurrect. When any ending or failure seems final, you may feel depressed, emotionally entombed. What you need is an empty grave, the sign that you are no longer in that deathly state but have come back to life.

But the empty tomb is not just a metaphor for getting back into life after loss or failure. It may also be support for the feeling that life doesn't end at death, that death is a transition to some other form of life. In this way, the empty tomb is like the grain manifested in the Greek Eleusinian Mysteries, reminding people that death and resurrection, like a seed planted in the earth, is a law of nature. So it is intelligent to have hope that death is not the final end. This is not knowledge or even belief. It is hope, plain and simple. The image of the empty tomb, without any explanation, directly gives you hope that life has its secrets, one of which might be an as-yet-inexplicable way onward.

Stop Trying

You become happy when you stop trying to be happy.
ZHUANGZI

❧

Pleasure, satisfaction, joy, good luck, cheerfulness — these are words the dictionary associates with happiness. People feel happy when things are going well and there is no dark cloud in the emotional sky to cause worry. "What, me worry?" said Alfred E. Neuman, of *Mad* magazine. He would not make a good advertisement for happiness, though. He looked more stupefied than cheerful. And so it is with happiness. Although some today study happiness seriously, there is a lightness in the concept that keeps it elusive. Happiness is so light that it's difficult to find its gravitas. Often it is a momentary sensation of well-being that doesn't have to be long-lived to be valued and prized. It's like a shooting star, or, in the words of Wallace Stevens, like "a pheasant disappearing in the brush."

Zhuangzi suggests that trying to be happy is exactly the wrong way to go about it. Of course, Taoists don't recommend *trying* to do anything. Their ideal is *wu-wei*, accomplishing much by doing nothing. Happiness can't be forced. You may go on a holiday to someplace special and try to be happy, but your plan may not work, because it is in the nature of happiness to simply occur, as a mood that settles rather than a state you can force into being. In this way, happiness is a gift of the gods or angels and cannot be manufactured.

Naturally, you can arrange life so that happiness is more likely, but it makes a difference not to force it or demand it. You set the scene and hope the angel of happiness will respond. It is the work of a special muse, like an inspiration to an artist. It may be the free gift of a daimon, an invisible force, inner and outer, that moves life onward or warns of danger. Aristotle's word for happiness is *eudaimonion*, "a good daimon."

The daimon doesn't appear very often, and neither does happiness. Happiness may be a passing sensation and not a continuing state. The ephemeral realization of happiness may be enough to sustain you. You get a dose of happiness like an electric jolt, and that juices you up until the next time it comes along. But the injection may spread and give you the feeling of a happy life.

All of this is to say that happiness, too, may be empty,

empty of our demands and control. More a mystery than a product, a gift rather than an achievement. Keep it empty, and its fullness may be available to you. Appreciate unhappiness as a legitimate and even valuable condition, and only then can you grasp happiness when it comes along.

Happiness may be more satisfying, as well, when it is part of a rhythm of challenge, sadness, and drudgery. Constant happiness would become dull and ineffective. It comes and goes, and that rhythm of presence and absence is part of its beauty. You wouldn't want unending happiness, because then you wouldn't know what you have — happiness is defined by its opposite. When sadness lifts or depression moves on, you feel happy just to have them gone.

Or you may come to realize that being happy often leads to some form of unhappiness. You may be thrilled to make some unexpected money. At first. Later you may discover the downside of being wealthy. You may get married in a state of bliss, and a year or so later crave a way out of the marriage. You may get a desirable job, and later realize that you were misled by promises of good fortune.

There is a kind of happiness that comes from good fortune or moments of peace and tranquility, especially the emotional kind. But another type of happiness appears when you are simply being who you are, in touch with your deeper laws, moving effortlessly without neurotic demands on yourself.

You don't try to attain this kind of happiness directly, but you can learn how life works and what your particular nature is and be careful not to violate these conditions. A deep happiness may arrive then, and it won't disappear when things go wrong or you occasionally feel sad. It settles in like a bright evening cloud with soft pink highlights. It infuses you, as though that same bright pink cloud is now inside you.

No Words Needed

You have a fishing pole so you can catch a fish. Once you get a fish, you don't need the pole.

You have a trap so you can catch a rabbit. Once you get a rabbit, you don't need the trap.

You use words to express meaning. Once you get the meaning, you don't need words.

I'd like to meet a person who has no more words so I can have a word with him.

Zhuangzi

⤜⤛

How do you have a word with someone who doesn't have any words? Do you stand together in silence, or do you speak words that are not yours? Maybe you use words that are not defined but float like poetry. When Robert Frost writes of a crossroads that he "took the one less traveled by," he is not talking about a road. He is talking about his life. So *road* doesn't mean "road." René Magritte made a painting of a pipe on which he placed front and center the words "This is not a pipe." Of course it's not a pipe. You can't smoke it. Just like you will never find the road that Frost took or the one he didn't take. This is not a road.

So, what are words if they don't mean what they are clearly describing? Words have a history and a personality and can be uttered poetically to mean something quite different from either the dictionary definition or the intention of the one using the word. Frost's poem is about how to live, not about a physical road.

The emptiness in a word may be its resistance to a limited definition or its deep historical etymology. For example, you may think that a restaurant is a place you go to eat well-cooked meals. But the word's root means "restore," which has a different connotation. You may want this word to mean what you want it to mean, but its history is clear. Before it was about good food, it was about restoring yourself. Get to know the words you have, and listen to what they want to say. The meanings will often differ from what people think they are saying.

If you are talking to people who don't have a set of fixed words that they insist on, you are free to express yourself. No jargon, no script, no ideology, no orthodoxy. Without this openness, these words are not empty, and for words to be freely used, they must be empty. Most groups have their own special words, and so do individual people. Some words are emotional, not empty. Some try to force you to a desired conclusion. Some are sly and manipulative. You should know when words thrown at you are not empty. Watch out!

An empty word is open to discussion and interpretation. It has no agendas hiding inside it like the warriors in the Trojan horse. For example, the word *religion* is a difficult one for me. I understand religion to be a way of life open to the infinite and mysterious. But the religions, and people who follow them, often mean just the opposite. For them, the word *religion* is not open and empty. It refers to an established belief system with a strong authoritative tradition. Depending on how it is used, *religion* can be one of the least empty words and the most rigid.

Words can lose their precious emptiness in many different ways, sometimes ad hoc, just for the occasion. Someone says he would like to have a conversation with me, but once it is underway, I discover that the conversation is actually an attempt to convert me to his way of thinking. I go from the possibility of empty words to the reality of words that have no emptiness in them at all. I look forward to a discussion, but I get a lecture aimed at forcing me to think in a certain way.

Walt Whitman empties words to the point that they are infinitely more intimate to us:

> Were you thinking that those were the words — those
>   upright lines? those curves, angles, dots?

No, those are not the words — the substantial words
 are in the ground and sea,
They are in the air — they are in you.

The words we read or speak are not the real words.
Real words lie hidden in the trees and streams.

An old sage once said, "Pardon me, may I have a word
with you?"

His companion replied, "I don't have any words, they
have me."

Words have power, and maybe their meaning doesn't
come from us. Look into the etymology of a single word.
You will see that history has shaped the word. You are under
the spell of history when you use it. James Hillman said
that words are angels, messengers, messages. He called for
an "angelology of words," angel specialists telling us about
words and their messages.

Many words used in everyday conversations are
coded, loaded with prejudice and expectation. Many
people have an agenda when they use words and pour
their ego anxieties into them. They wonder if the person in front of them is politically conservative or liberal,
religious or secular, feminist or gay or environmentalist.
In all these cases, I am with Zhuangzi with a twist: Show
me a person who has empty words so I can have a word
with him.

How Many Tigers

One day the leader in his village asked Nasrudin to go hunting for tigers. Nasrudin felt he had to go, but he didn't want to. When he returned, his friends asked him, "How did it go?"

"Excellent," he said.

"How many tigers did you kill?"

"None."

"How many did you encounter?"

"None."

"How many did you see?"

"None."

"Why do you say the hunt was excellent if you didn't see even one tiger?"

"When you're hunting tigers, none is plenty."

It sometimes happens that you get very involved in looking for something, when it would be better if you gave up the hunt altogether. Once, when I was a young man, I didn't know what my future would be. I felt I needed a job that was suited to my talents. So I applied for a position as a writer of training manuals for a large insurance company. As a test they asked me to write a manual for anything at all, just to show my skills. So I wrote a very clear booklet on how a pipe organ works. This was something I knew about.

The company's hiring officer was shrewd. "You've done an excellent job," he said. "But you seem to be a real writer. We need someone who can just write a training manual well and has no aspirations as a writer. Sorry, we can't hire you." His logic was clear but a bit twisted: "We are looking for someone who can write well.... You are a good writer, so we can't hire you."

It's a good thing I didn't get that job. It would have killed my spirit. Not getting the job left me empty, open for a marvelous career that was waiting for me. In those days, if someone inquiring about my quest for my life work had asked, "Do you have any good leads?" I could have answered, "None is plenty."

There are several important life lessons in this simple story. For example, when you're looking for something that you want badly, if you come up empty, that may be the best outcome. It's often better not to get what you desire. For one thing, you may not see that the object of your quest is not good for you in the long run, no matter how strong your desire is. You may not see the big picture and focus only on a narrow goal. You might also learn that a desire fulfilled can block other possibilities. If you literalize one desire by indulging in it, you may interfere with others yet to come. A friend asks, "Did you ever find that job you were looking for?" "No," you say, "I found a different job, and it turned out to be the perfect job, one I didn't know I was looking for."

Notice that Nasrudin is not at all dismayed not to have even seen a tiger on his hunt. He is trained in emptiness and knows how to see the value in not finding even a trace of what he is searching for. Maybe the hunt is enough, without success in any conventional sense.

In my life I made serious efforts to be a priest, a musician, a college professor. In the end I became a bestselling author and world-traveling lecturer, neither of which I'd ever aspired to. I never hunted for those roles, but that is what I got. Fortunately, my early goals didn't stop me from continuing my search. The job I got was not the one I was looking for, but the job I got was worth more to me than anything I could have sought.

My friend John trained hard to become an engineer and got a job at a small college. But then he was attracted by the work of the school chaplain and studied to become a theologian. Then he took a position as a pastor of a church. That didn't work, so he became a trained and skilled psychotherapist. John often told me that he felt he was an engineer at heart, though he was glad he had become a therapist. Originally he had hunted for the life of a scientist, but there he came up empty. He felt fulfilled doing therapy, the tiger he had always been looking for.

Another way to see this perceptive story is to remember that the journey may be more important than the goal. As the Greek poet Cavafy says in his famous poem "Ithaca," our goal keeps us on the journey, even if in the end it is disappointing:

> Ithaca has given you the beautiful voyage....
> But she has nothing more to give you.

The Empty Pot

It was time for the emperor to retire and find a successor. To all the children of his empire he gave a pot full of rich, dark earth. "I have placed a seed in each pot," he told the children. "Tend the pots, and the one who shows me the most beautiful and healthy plant will become ruler. I will look at the pots in four months' time."

Jun took his pot home and put it in a place in the sun and watered it daily and talked to it kindly. But it didn't grow. Not one shoot of green broke through the earth. He tended it for four months, and nothing happened. Then it was the day to face the emperor.

Jun took his pot to the palace and joined a throng of other children with their pots. Immediately he saw that their pots were overflowing with stems and leaves of rich green plants standing tall and brilliant. The emperor came and looked at all the fertile pots and said to the children, "I boiled all those seeds. None of them should have come up. But look, there is only one empty pot. You others obviously replaced the seed I gave you with new seeds and tried to outwit your emperor. But here Jun

has come honestly and courageously with an empty pot, and he
will be your new emperor."

It isn't easy to endure emptiness, even if it is of the mysterious and otherworldly kind. Everyone wants fullness and completion and success. It isn't easy to endure failure, even if it is honest. It isn't easy to disappoint with your emptiness and absence. But if that is indeed what you have, failure and emptiness, that is what you bring. You carry your emptiness, whatever it is, with grace.

This is one of the basic rules of life: Know how to bear the gaps and challenges. The children who put new seeds in their pots couldn't bear bringing them to the emperor without a plant in them. Sometimes you simply have to hold on to failure instead of excusing it or finding a way to cover it over. Facing emptiness has its rewards.

Mysteriously, emptiness may define who you are and contribute to the fulfillment of your life. You may spend the energy of your life trying to avoid the gaps and inadequacies, but that avoidance makes you miss your mark.

The ancient Chinese story of the empty pot teaches us to accept the imperfections that life has given us. To deny them or pretend they do not exist may offer a momentary ego stroke but ultimately it keeps us from enjoying the reward of being in charge of our lives. To be an emperor in your life, you have to appreciate the nothingness when it pops up.

The image of the planted pot also points to the idea of growth. We would like to see our lives grow, as though they were plants just needing water and sunshine and plenty of care. But maybe growth isn't the only important value. Maybe it is important that some of our potential doesn't materialize. Maybe we need dead ends and failed opportunities. Maybe they are part of the whole picture of our being.

Development and maturing may not be the absolute values we think they are. James Hillman used to say that there is a maternal fantasy behind the very idea of human development. Like a child, we expect continuous growth and are disappointed or even alarmed if we don't feel we are developing properly. We are not trees; we are human beings, he said. But maybe there are other deep fantasies of human life besides development and growth that are also valuable. Think of the lives of artists and scientists who ran into periods of blockages and overwhelming obstacles, how these fallow moments inspired new ideas or at least were an important part of the whole picture.

In our tale, the emperor is shrewd. He knows that following the rules and succeeding are not necessarily signs of a good potential leader. An emperor must also know the value of not growing and not being successful. At a deeper level of the tale, we might understand that for us to be successful at life, we need to nurture nongrowth and failure as well as growth and success.

It would be better to incorporate emptiness in all its forms into our conception of life. We need to tend our empty pots and not be embarrassed about the fact that there is nothing in them. Not growing may serve a purpose. If someone asks you, "What's happening in your life?" you may answer, "Not much." That simple affirmation of emptiness may mature you to the point where you can live your complexity. Not feeling compelled to display your success, your leafy growing plant, is an alternative to the demand to always manifest the big green leaves of success.

FORGETFULNESS

I became water
  and saw myself
      a mirage
became an ocean
    saw myself a speck
        of foam
gained Awareness
    saw that all is but
          forgetfulness
woke up
    and found myself
        asleep.

This disappearing poem by Binavi Badakhshâni, an Afghan
Sufi, portrays emptiness as a slide out of being. Just when

you think you have got something, it slips away or becomes its opposite.

To see that you are a mirage — what a discovery, the opposite of the myth of Narcissus, who finds himself in water. You may look at your reflection and see nothing. Is the self a mirage? Is the very sense of being a person a fantasy, a provisional realization that vanishes upon reflection? Or is the sensation of being an individual less important than we think? Is our purpose on the planet more to be a contributor to the human community than to stand out as a separate thing?

Over a lifetime you get a grand view of life and your place in it, and yet this poem says that big vision turns into a speck of foam in the ocean. Maybe to have a big life, which is certainly a valuable aspiration, only works if you also see yourself as a speck. Alchemists used the phrase, "bigger than big, smaller than small." A contradiction? Maybe not. More like a seesaw that requires two equal sides to make the game fun.

You become aware only to discover that in the flux of life you forget what you were aware of. You need forgetfulness as much as you need awareness. The object of discovery must sink into the muck of what you know and what you have become. Emily Dickinson asks: "Is it oblivion or absorption when things pass from our minds?"

The ancient Greeks honored the River Lethe, the river of forgetfulness that souls must cross on their way to Hades. You forget your past life to prepare for the one to come. And maybe this is not to be taken literally to describe afterlife but a pattern within life. Is it more a rhythm of remembering and forgetting, becoming aware and not remembering what you were aware of? Maybe it is all right to live a life of absolute forgetfulness and let whatever the source of this life may be do the remembering.

Awareness necessarily fades into forgetfulness so that awareness can rise once again. It is the wave of awareness followed by a wave of forgetfulness that keeps the imagination fluid and alive. You don't cling to your awareness, because that would stop the flow and the rhythm. You enjoy the moment of awareness, and then you forget it.

The most difficult lesson is to realize that finally waking up after years of dormancy and unconsciousness is not actually the achievement you thought it was. Waking up is a goal worth pursuing, but you will be led astray if you don't realize that this new waking up is only the occasion for more sleep. The Buddha is not only the Awakened One; he is also the Sleeping One, the one who lies prone with his head on his hand.

We have many depictions of the Buddha as the Awakened One but also of the sleeping Buddha, sometimes called the reclining Buddha or the Buddha entering nirvana. We have an image of Jesus asleep — in a boat with his followers in the middle of a storm. In their anxiety they wake him up, and he calms the weather. Spiritual masters know when not to be awake and alert.

The tale of Jesus asleep in the boat teaches us to find

peace and relaxation as our mode of being in the storms of everyday life. We can wake up and go into action, if necessary, to calm the storm, but our normal position is to be asleep wherever we are. We hear a lot about awareness and waking up, but not enough about sleeping as a way of being.

Many people are interested in consciousness and becoming more conscious. Some want to be conscious of their dreams and enjoy lucid dreaming, where they can affect the outcome of the dream. They speak of consciousness as a great achievement.

But maybe *conscious* is not the best word. Maybe we should be as unconscious during the day as we are asleep at night. You go to a psychotherapist sometimes thinking that if you can figure yourself out, you will have an easier life. Then you discover that understanding may not have the impact you expected. You know why you are doing something that gives you pain, but you still can't stop doing it.

Instead of awareness and consciousness you may need an approach that is midway between waking and sleeping or that consists of both. This is where imagination and images come into play. If you can find someone with whom you can tell your story and feel heard, that may be more effective than turning to someone who will give you an explanation for what is going on.

Sleep is largely dreaming, and it is the dream that gives real insight into the dramas playing out in life. You may have to be dreamier rather than more analytical. Life might be more pleasurable if you were to live in a dream state than if you try hard to be awake and aware.

Finally, you wake up. Like the Buddha, you become an awakened one. You get up from the tomb, like Jesus. You resurrect. But, as before, you find that you are asleep. Resurrection and sleep keep going on, time and time again, in a rhythm that defines a good life. You must find yourself asleep so you can resurrect and become an awakened being. You must keep getting up so you can sink into the sleep of unconsciousness. The whole of life is like a normal day — waking and sleeping, sleeping and waking.

GONE AWAY

One summer day I visited, but the master had gone
    somewhere.
Only a lotus blossom
arranged in a vase
guardian of the hermitage,
its fragrance
filling the room.
TEISHIN

Ryokan (1758–1831) was a celebrated Japanese Zen poet and calligrapher. When he was sixty-eight he met the Zen nun Teishin, who was forty years younger than him. They became friends and exchanged poems in a creative dialogue between two poets.

Here, she visits but discovers that the master is not

there. She sees a flower arrangement and smells the fragrance that fills the room. This moment is like the one in the Gospel when Jesus's followers come to find his body in the tomb after his execution. But the tomb is empty. Here, too, the master is gone, and yet the room is filled with something invisible but perceptible. To the eyes the room is empty, but to the nose something is definitely there.

Some things may appear empty and yet from another point of view are full. One year, my family wanted to downsize and move to a smaller house on a small lake in New England. My wife and daughter vetted several houses and then showed me the ones that interested them. They said, "There is one other one that we don't think is a possibility. It looks like a construction site, and it's covered in plastic shingles and railings." But we went to look at it anyway. I saw a well-built house in a beautiful setting in need of cosmetic changes. We ended up buying it and doing some gardening and making a few adjustments to the building. Its fullness was revealed, and we have been enjoying this house for many years now. It was empty, waiting for its completion. You have to see what is not visible. The master is not at home, but the fragrance of the blossoms he left there fills the house. When I saw that house, I smelled something.

This story is a metaphor for life. Emptiness can be an invitation to an increase of life's intensity and pleasure. You take a new job, and at first it feels worthless, until you smell its hidden virtues. Plain eyesight can be misleading. Other senses may tell you more: intuition, memory, foresight, and imagination.

This poem may teach you that at the very moment you think something is empty, that is a good time to use your "nose" and smell out something good. Look for what no one sees. Pay attention to the invisibles.

Emptiness doesn't have to be complete. Near emptiness may be enough. Or something that looks empty but really is not. Spotting emptiness is usually a signal to stay where you are, explore, consider the possibilities. If no one is home, you may smell the flowers.

I once wanted very much to see a tapestry of Hermes Trismegistus, a rare and often-replicated image, in the cathedral in Siena, Italy. I assumed I would be in Siena only once in my life. The day I visited, the tapestry was covered over to prevent its fading in the sunlight. There was no possibility of making it visible. But having gone to this cathedral, I discovered an underground, ancient, and highly original museum across the piazza, which presented in much greater potency the mystery I had hoped to glimpse in the cathedral. Sometimes, when someone does not show up or a place is closed for the day, it is a sign to use your nose, sniff out other possibilities, and maybe find your wishes fulfilled.

ROTTING BAMBOO

The Zen nun Chiyono studied Zen and practiced meditation for a
long time without getting anywhere. One night, when the moon
was big, she carried water in an old bucket bound with bamboo.
The bamboo broke and the bottom of the bucket fell off, and in
that instant Chiyono was liberated.

   To mark the moment, she wrote this poem:

   I did everything to keep the bucket
   from breaking
   because the bamboo was rotting
   and would soon give out.
   Finally the bottom gave way.
   No water in the bucket.
   No moon in the water.

How many aspects of our lives have run their course, but we keep at them anyway? Some things are not so significant: an old, frayed shirt in a closet or a pair of shoes with holes in them. Other things are highly significant: a rusting career or relationship. We keep them and probably don't realize how they stop up the flow of life in general. Clear out some old clothes, and feel the lightness in your heart. Let go of a job that is no longer appropriate for you, and notice the bounce in your gait.

The nun in the story is not only carrying a bucket that is coming apart. She is bearing the weight of water and the reflection of the moon. That is all too much to carry. It is the same with larger life issues. You carry around something that is no longer viable, and it's like holding a world in your hands. Often, when you get rid of something that is coming undone, some other thing, huge and onerous, will also go away.

The Zen spirit involves letting go of things that are no longer worth your effort. Often you don't need to add something to your experience, such as a new teacher, community, or book. You may need to let go of what you have that no longer has life in it. Often it is more difficult to let go than to hold on, and we hold on because we think that having is more important than losing.

Important and precious things do get old and fall apart. The house you have been living in may no longer be appropriate and meaningful. You can let it go and allow life to move on. The way you have been eating may not be healthy at this new time in your life. Let it go and try a new way. The way you spend your holidays and leisure time may be showing its limitations. It may be time to try something new. Let it go. Don't carry it around any longer. Always try to see the bamboo rotting.

Something of greater meaning may be reflected in your habits. You may be doing certain things because your family did them and you know them from childhood. This kind of repetition can become a deep and heavy habit. Remember that Freud said that certain repetitions signal the death instinct rather than life. You may feel the rot and death in those habits, and now you can let go of them and allow life to flow.

You may have ideas and opinions that are getting old and frayed. It may be time to release them. Good ideas are alive, and grow and change. If you carry them with you too long, it's as if the moon itself is on your back. Notice that these ideas are rotting, and let them die off in their own time. Let them go. You don't have to wait for their bottoms to give out.

Knowing Not-Knowing

It is only when we forget all our learning that we begin to know. I do not get nearer by a hair's breadth to any natural object so long as I presume that I have an introduction to it from some learned man. To conceive of it with a total apprehension I must for the thousandth time approach it as something totally strange.

HENRY DAVID THOREAU

It is a good idea to forget many of the things you have learned over the years. Some are outmoded, some incorrect, some too obvious and trite. We also need a fresh approach to things of interest, to see them as if for the first time, to attain "beginner's mind." This approach would help make a thing "strange."

Years ago, when I kept coming across the idea that knowledge is not a good thing, I used to wonder if this was anti-intellectualism. But I kept finding the idea in the work of many brilliant thinkers that I admired. I loved to read and study, and I knew they did. So why were they so negative about knowledge? Here is poet David Hinton's translation of chapter 71 of the Tao Te Ching:

> Knowing not-knowing is lofty.
> Not knowing not-knowing is affliction.

Let me go over this beautiful translation as I understand it: If you know the importance of not knowing everything, or anything for that matter, you are way ahead. You know the most important thing. If you don't appreciate the importance of not knowing everything, you are going to have problems. You will be under the dangerous illusion that you know what life is all about. You will have banished the mysteries that are so important. You will be full of ego, thinking that you know what you are talking about, when in fact you are only defending against your ignorance. The starting point toward wisdom is to acknowledge your basic ignorance, your not-knowing.

Let's delve into Zen master Shunryu Suzuki's phrase "beginner's mind." You can always find a frame of mind in which you are a beginner, maybe once again. You keep coming back to the role of student and novice, open to learning because there is something you know you do not know. How fruitful that attitude is. But you could discover it in any situation, acknowledging and appreciating the extent to which you don't know something. Sometimes achieving it may require a little bruising to the ego, but that is always a good thing.

When you cultivate not-knowing along with learning, you also allow room for mystery, for the profound and inexplicable parts of life that give you a sense of awe. An appreciation of the unknowable keeps you honest and humble in the best way. It is the base of a religious or spiritual attitude and in the end makes you more human. The truly wise person knows how important it is not to know everything.

I sometimes find myself giving a lecture or speaking in an interview when I know I don't know at all what I am talking about. Usually that is because the topic is unknowable. I often speak about the soul, for instance, yet after years of study I still don't know just what the soul is. They ask me to talk about God, and I'm certainly at a loss there.

The trouble with some teachers and leaders is not that they don't know what they are talking about, but that they don't know that they don't know what they are talking about. They go on blissfully using words that even they do not really understand, but they think they do, or at least talk as if they do.

The solution is to admit to our ignorance and try to clear our minds of preconceptions. These are Thoreau's recommendations. Try to forget what you think you know. Don't rely on authorities, but simply be in the presence of whatever it is you are concerned with. Finally, aim for "total comprehension" and not just acquaintance.

As I sometimes put it, knowledge from the soul is more intimate than knowledge from research and study. Both are valuable, but Thoreau is reminding us of an approach we may overlook: being closely present to the thing we are studying. I sometimes listen to professors giving speeches about psychotherapy, and yet they have never practiced it. I have been doing it for forty years and sense an important gap in their presentations, a wide gap. I do not want to say that you always have to have an experience of something before you can comment on it. Sometimes a good distance is useful. Still, there is some valuable emptiness in forgetting your information and just being present with the object of your investigation.

THE LOST BOWL

A little boy in China goes with his mother and aunts to a Buddhist temple in the mountains. He takes part in a ritual and asks many questions about the monks and nuns. A monk gives him a beautiful blue bowl that is so precious to the boy that he puts it next to his pillow as he sleeps on the last night of his visit.

The next morning he rushes to get to the boat to take him and his family home and forgets the bowl. Once he boards the boat he realizes he doesn't have it and refuses to leave. A worker on the boat runs up the mountain, delaying departure considerably, and brings the bowl back to the boy. Then the boy plays with the bowl on the side of the boat and accidentally drops it in the water and watches it float away. He is upset, but his mother tells him to eat something and stop thinking about it. She says, "Such things won't be rare occurrences in the future."

Later in life, the boy, now a man, says, "Looking back, I find my mother's words an ominous prophecy. Such things are indeed no rare occurrences in my life. Many things and people, far more precious than that bowl, have been lost. Some broken.

At that moment, with the floating bowl, only my childhood vanished."
MU XIN

∾

Every life is loaded with loss, from the death of a parent or grandparent to the end of a marriage to the disappearance of good health. The poignancy in this childhood story of losing a blue bowl may remind you that loss stirs emotions that not only are painful but also give life its value. I wish my mother and father were still here for a warm and fun conversation, but missing them reminds me how precious life is and how important it is to be available to my friends and family members.

Sometimes the whole of life is compressed and summarized in a single, apparently insignificant event, like losing a bowl on a childhood excursion. We could reflect on experiences that come and go. They are like fractals, tiny events that contain the big secrets of life in miniature form.

At first, the boy makes a special effort to retrieve the bowl, holding up a crowd of people eager to get home. The people have been delayed, the bowl appears, and then it is lost in the water for good, floating away. A double loss, two times empty.

We keep making efforts to hang on to things that seem important to us at the time: a job, a relationship, a home, some important ideas. We lose them and make a big fuss about the loss. Only later do we discover what a loss it truly was, and then we lose these same precious things again.

The Greeks said that the god Hermes was a thief. He is that aspect of life that takes away. Life is not always so giving. It causes us to lose things that seem important. If we didn't lose things, we would never move along in life, which is a series of changes, gains and losses. The joy of presence and the pain of loss: These two waves of emotion keep us going. Hermes the Thief, the cause of painful loss, is a kind god who offers humans a good life.

This is a little boy's story, and it has the ring of a rite of passage. The boy has to learn this lesson about loss because it will be applied often in his adult life. The lesson involves a loss of innocence, the idea that life is always positive and giving. That is not the way it is. You will suffer losses that will be difficult to understand and tolerate. At some time in your life you will have to learn this basic lesson: No matter how hard you try to keep loss out of your life, it will happen. You may come to respect loss, and even in the midst of the pain it brings, you may see its place in the scope of things.

The bowl was blue. Light blue? Sky blue? The place where we find the sun. An old American song says, "Please don't take my sunshine away." John Updike wrote a poignant short story about a little boy who loses his innocence at a carnival, where a man working a booth cheats him of a few coins. The song plays in the background as the older man betrays the innocent young child. In our story, the boy loses his bowl after finding it. This shade of blue, like the pure sky, is no longer available to him. He has to grow up and lose the joys of plain innocence.

But the little boy and girl live in us all our lives, and we are forever losing another remnant of innocence. We are always growing up. Always losing our blue bowl, our clear blue sky and sunshine. That's just how life is, an essential rhythm of weightless innocence and heavy loss. Life empties, even more than it fills.

No One in the Boat

When I was young, my grandfather would take me on a Sunday onto a small Michigan lake in a little rowboat to fish or just enjoy the water. Just the two of us. One day, when I was four years old, we took our little boat trip on a larger lake, Lake St. Clair, just north of Detroit, where my aunt and uncle had a home on the water.

We were about fifty yards away from the shore in deep, choppy water, when suddenly I felt cold water crawling up my legs. Then the boat turned over in the water, and then from a short distance from the boat I saw cushions and baskets and a gasoline can floating on the surface. I was gasping for breath and felt my grandfather's strong arms lift me up onto the surface of the upturned boat. Then I went unconscious. Before I blacked out, I saw my uncle dive off the cement dock in front of his house into the water in a heroic effort to save us.

When I awoke I was lying in an unfamiliar bed that seemed to me like a giant's bed, it was so big, and the sheets and blankets were stretched tightly across my shoulders. I heard the word undertaker whispered by someone in the room, and

I decided I must be dead. But it was my grandfather who had drowned.

One of the lessons I learned from that life-shaping experience was the meaning of courage and selflessness. Thirty years later, in an intense therapy session, I was able to open up to my tears of gratitude and feel the stronger force of that generous act. I learned, too, what being a father and grandfather means and what it implies to be "a man of heart." I never say a word against men in general, as many today do, because I have witnessed what a man in touch with his deep and genuine manliness can be and do.

I can still see those cans and cushions floating in the cold water. Often they appear in my memory whenever I am trying to swim or enjoy rowing in my small boat today. I can still sense the odd touch of the overturned boat, now hollow and useless. That boat was supposed to keep us safe as we simply enjoyed a Sunday afternoon in the sun on friendly waters. But the empty boat taught me a major lesson, that life is full of threats and shadows, and you should be vigilant at all times, ready for a turn in fortune and a sudden withdrawal of the beauty and protection of the natural world.

In many cultures young men and women go through rituals that help them grow up and learn the harsh lessons of life. They might be buried for a day or two under a pile of leaves or in a shallow hollow in the land to remind them of the reality of death and the two-sided morality of nature: It can sustain you and it can kill you.

I didn't need a ritual burial to become familiar with death. The empty boat on a choppy lake transformed me, at least in part, from a too-trusting child into a more realistic young man. The rough, fathomless lake initiated me toward young adulthood and did so from its cold heart. After all, I first felt its encroachment that day as a chill rising up my ankles and legs. It presented itself first in its coldness, such a contrast to the warmth of my family and especially my doting grandfather.

When I think of this sad but memorable event, I wonder about my grandfather being prepared for the moment when he could give his life for the child in his care. I imagine being ready for that kind of moment in my own life, and the older I get, the more I admire courage. It is easy to talk about but not so easy to conjure up when needed.

This is real love, not so emotional and not sentimental. A cool love that matches the cold waters of nature and the cool demands of fate. It is also family love, grandfather love. We all have to learn the difficult lesson that every human being is family, and we should all be ready to give our lives for another, to empty ourselves on behalf of the younger people about to take our place in life.

THE HEART SUTRA

Quan Yin
was deep into the practice of attaining wisdom
when she understood that the five skandas —
physical existence, sensing, perceiving, thinking,
and awareness — are empty.
At that she was relieved of suffering and anxiety.

Dear Sariputra,
whatever you perceive is empty
because perception itself is empty.
To be visible is to be empty,
because vision is empty.
It's the same for
sensing, perceiving,
having impressions, and being aware.

Dear Sariputra,
All objects and everything visible have this quality
of emptiness:

They are neither visible nor invisible,
pure nor impure,
getting bigger nor getting smaller.
In emptiness there is no such thing as
grasping what is visible
or sensing, perceiving, having impressions, or being aware.

There are no eyes, ears, nose, tongue, body, or mind;
no sights, sounds, odors, tastes, things to touch, or thoughts;
no ignorance and no end of ignorance;
nor is there any aging or dying
and yet there is no end of aging and dying;
no suffering, acquiring, ending, or having a path;
no wisdom and no getting anywhere.
Since you can't get anywhere,
bodhisattvas depend on prajna-paramita,
which is achieving a level of deep understanding.
Their thinking is free of blocks.
Since they are free of blocks,
they are not afraid.
Free of confusing illusions,
they live in a state of nirvana.

All buddhas of the past, present, and future,
relying on prajna-paramita,
reach complete fulfillment.
So, understand: praising prajna-paramita
is the wonderful transcendent mantra,
the highest mantra,
the perfectly embracing mantra
that can eliminate suffering.
Prajna-Paramita is real, not an illusion.

So chant the prajna-paramita *mantra,*
the mantra that goes:

not here, absent,
not here at all,
truly absent.

This is wisdom.
Beautiful!

With the Heart Sutra, we come to the very essence of emptiness. This remarkable prayer depicts a way of life based on principles very different from modern thinking, a way of life in which emptiness in its many forms colors everything you do. These principles may sound quite odd to a modern person, who understands adding to life but not taking away. They do not make much sense in a literal, practical, and ordinary world. No one today wants to live a life without understanding.

"Without understanding" doesn't mean you should not try to understand day-to-day activities, such as how to pay your bills. It means that there are some things, the most important truths, that can never be fully understood. Eventually you need to confront these imponderables.

Also, in the most important matters, you don't want to be attached to any system or teaching or community.

You have to find an "empty" way of learning, seeking community, and developing a philosophy of life.

The word *empty* saturates the Heart Sutra so that, in the end, this celebrated confession of nonattachment empties itself. It is not like anything else. It makes emptiness absolute, while insisting that there are no absolutes. The word *empty* pounds throughout the sutra so many times that it leaves you no attachments, nothing to hold tightly. In the end, it is all gone, completely gone. You are left with a nothingness that you have achieved through careful labor and attention.

In the Heart Sutra *empty* means many things: not being attached, not taking things literally, not believing rigidly in anything, not acting on ideas you might be too devoted to, not preaching, not getting stuck on a teacher or a teaching, always being in a swirl of change, not making progress, or not not making progress. You can go in this vein in your own way, making your own list. We are all empty in our own ways.

But here is a key: Emptiness here does not mean vacancy. It is not a problem and is not usually associated with pain. In that way it is not heartbreaking loss but rather an odd opportunity to be fully present and therefore not vacant at all. It is part of a paradox, where fullness and emptiness sustain each other. Don't be attached, and suddenly your life opens into possibility. Even if you subscribe to a philosophy of life or a psychology that is persuasive, keep it empty. Don't give it everything. Don't turn it into an ideology, which may be a philosophy of life too dense, fixed, and rigid.

The Heart Sutra puts a blanket of emptiness over all experiences. Everything is empty, with no exceptions. All your beliefs, attachments, pride, ownership, feelings of virtuousness, the sense of being right, your value-laden actions — all of them must be empty, or else the ego creeps in to spoil some aspect of your efforts. That means that in some often-undetectable ways they become neurotic.

To be truly effective, your ideas and behavior need to be clear of ego, not spoiled by even small narcissistic needs or infantile habits that rise out of fear of failure or any need to be seen as perfect. The realization of your inherent imperfection keeps you honest and emotionally clear. You can make a mistake and know that you always have more to learn.

The Heart Sutra speaks to the very essence of what it means to be a human being, and for that reason it is chanted and written out every day all over the world. It would be good for modern Westerners to adopt this practice and learn calligraphy, or chant, or illustrate the sutra with drawings, or extend it with personal poetry. Tradition teaches that it requires daily attention and working through so that it does in fact affect one's daily life.

THE ABSENT GOD

God would have us know that we must live as people who manage our lives without him. The God who is with us is the God who forsakes us (Mark 15:34). The God who lets us live in the world without the working hypothesis of God is the God before whom we stand continually. Before God and with God we live without God.

DIETRICH BONHOEFFER

～～

When Hitler rose to power, Dietrich Bonhoeffer was a Christian pastor studying and teaching at Union Theological Seminary in New York. In 1939, when the situation became tense, Bonhoeffer went back to Germany and took part in a plot to kill Hitler. The conspirators were discovered and condemned to death by hanging. He spent two years in prison and then was executed.

While in prison Bonhoeffer worked out his theological ideas about ethics and a world-focused approach to the spiritual life in his letters. Our quote here is one of several examples in that vein. He once said that he felt uncomfortable when people around him talked about "God." He knew they didn't mean what he meant by the word.

If any word should be empty, it is the word *God*. If you want to preserve the essential mysticism of the divine, to keep it holy, ineffable, and unknown, then you can't use the word indiscriminately. In fact, the louder and more frequently you use the word, the more it loses its power to denote the infinite and the awe-inspiring. Those many traditions that prohibit the use of the word *God* have a good point: If you keep using this word, it will lose its power to evoke the infinite, and then you will stray into idolatry and profanity. Bonhoeffer's beautiful and careful positioning of God helps you keep your religious awe and devotion without making God into a superhuman being and anthropomorphizing "Him." God is so far beyond your conceiving and control that it is entirely inappropriate to use the word *God* in a familiar manner.

Bonhoeffer leaves us in a paradox: "Before God and with God we live without God." The word *God* is an annihilating force. Rather than give us a puppet stand-in for the divine, it wipes out any solid, sure, controllable definition of who God is. Now the word serves a different and unusual purpose: to abolish any certainty you have or can expect from a name. Instead of certainty, the word serves emptiness.

Imagine if you could train yourself to hear the word *God* as a kind of emptiness, a name for what is present, but not physically. Bonhoeffer wants us to return to a world that is complete in itself, with no need for an otherworldly reality. At the same time, he doesn't want us to fall into secularism, a belief that God does not exist. Secularism is stifling. There is no exit. We need God, and yet he has to remain in the silent spaces between words and in those moments when we can't find the right word.

Bonhoeffer wants it both ways: God, no God. The more you try to explain this, the more convoluted the whole process becomes. And yet this is an important formulation: We can't live in a closed universe, but we can't live in a universe where God is present. The only way to do both is to live in this paradox of paradoxes, this empty "truth."

Sacred Ignorance

I followed the paths of many different teachings to get here and was unsuccessful until one day, while I was at sea on my way back from Greece, I was led to an insight through, as I would put it, the immeasurable generosity of the father of lights, from whom the best gifts always come. I was overwhelmed with the uncomprehending knowledge of educated ignorance. I had to go beyond eternal truths grasped in normal human fashion. Now that I have spelled out this idea, which is also true, in two books, Educated Ignorance *and* Conjectures, *I can give it focus and expand it.*

NICHOLAS OF CUSA

Nicholas of Cusa (1401–1464) was the James Joyce of theologians, forever making up new words and speaking in mind-bending imagery. In the quotation above, he writes about "uncomprehending knowledge." What is that? Knowing without understanding? *Educated Ignorance*, the title of his most famous work, is in itself an oxymoron, two words that cancel each other out. Elsewhere, in Latin, he crushes together *posse*, "to be possible," with *est*, "it is." *Possest* means something is possible and at the same time, is.

Another book, *Conjectures*, offers a provisional solution to a problem that may or may not be right and effective. Most of Nicholas's key words have this hollow ring of emptiness in them, and that is their value and beauty. They offer an idea and then take it away. They increase your ignorance, which is what he, as a teacher, tried to do.

He praised *sacra ignorantia*, sacred ignorance. An empty head, perhaps. Not thinking. Not intellectualizing everything. Having no definitions or explanations for things. Experiencing the world without figuring it out, by letting it come into you and by being present to it. Emptying yourself by becoming lost in the infinite cosmos or by the infinite butting into your contemplation.

Nicholas said that thinking you understand the infinite ground of things is like looking at a polygon, a shape made up of lines and angles, from a distance and perceiving it to be a circle. Up close, you see straight lines and angles. It has no curves but offers the illusion of a perfectly round circle. I used to draw these forms when I was a high school student. You think, Nicholas said, that you have seen the infinite and know it, but your knowledge is an illusion and is far from perfect. You may be fortunate enough to discover your basic ignorance, and that would be an advance.

Each of us should know, Nicholas taught, exactly where and how we are personally ignorant. It's not just a cultural matter or an issue for human beings in general. We each have our own kind of ignorance, and we can make it a life goal to discover what it is — perhaps a complete lack of understanding about the possibility of an infinite presence or intelligence at work in the cosmos or, certainly related, about what happens after we die.

To live in a soulless, mechanical world explained away by materialistic science is not a good option, and yet it is insanely popular today. Don't people sense the many mysteries that fill contemporary experience, the unanswered questions, the uncanny things that happen in life, and the many intelligent people of the past who experienced strange and mysterious events? Is it definite that there is no personal existence after death? Have all the billions of people who have lived on earth trusting in an afterlife been wrong?

I have been in some form of school for seventy-five years. In my old age I am learning how to be ignorant.

Not Owning

One day Abu Muhammad, a friend and student of the Sufi master Abu Sa'id, went to visit him at a bathhouse.

"Do you like this place?" the sheikh asked.

"Yes, very much," Abu Muhammad replied.

"Why?"

"Because you're here."

"No, really."

"Because all you need is a jug to pour water on your body and a towel to dry off, and these things belong to the bathhouse."

MOJDEH BAYAT AND MOHAMMAD ALI JAMNIA

༺ ༻

I spent my years thirteen to twenty-six in a Catholic religious order, the Servites, living an intense way of life under vows of chastity, poverty, and obedience. We lived the life seriously, devotedly, and happily. Chastity, as I understood it, didn't mean giving up your sexuality or repressing it; it meant not living an active sexual life and not having a special emotional relationship with another. This important vow, like the others, served the spirit of community. Obedience meant doing what the authorities of the community decided was best for the community. It meant paying attention to what the community needed, and surrendering your own needs. Poverty did not mean living without necessities but toning down ownership and extravagance. My mates and I shared even our personal things.

Not owning a pitcher of water and a towel at the bath would be a typical and characteristic situation in my community then, and that attitude lent the life a lightness and easing of ego, as well as a feeling of community. I learned through daily experience that emptying life of its possessions and its possessiveness can be freeing. There might be moments when I would wish to own a radio or a typewriter (this was before computers), but the vow wouldn't have meant much without the occasional pinch of our kind of poverty.

I feel that these vows that once taught me how to live in a community are still with me as a father and husband. I'm happy to share the things the family owns, and often I prefer to see my daughter, son, or wife enjoy some new purchase rather than possess it myself. Almost daily I remember my continuing vow of poverty.

But family isn't the only area where you can practice

the spirit of poverty. In general, you can stop seeing possessions as a measure of success or happiness. You can simplify and tone down the elegance in your life. You can make do with simpler arrangements in your home or be selective in how you fill your life with things. William Morris, a utopian and social reformer, said you should get rid of anything you have that is not beautiful. That is one way to simplify.

The imaginative social critic Ivan Illich supported a strong sense of the "commons" — land, buildings, and objects reserved for community use, such as parks and transportation. This is not communism, which is extreme and total, but a humane and moderate sharing of certain resources for the common good.

I know from experience that a toning down of elegance and extravagance contributes to a meaningful and pleasurable life. This kind of emptiness makes life richer and more enjoyable. It offers an alternative to the compulsive longing for things and gadgets and distracting electronics.

I recommend that everyone take a vow of poverty, just to tone down your cravings and create a simpler life. You can do this even with a moderate or high income. You could be more generous with your money and time and devote less attention to personal acquisition. Your spirit and soul will benefit. Like going to the bath, not just to get clean but to relax and get healthy, while not owning anything you need for the bath.

MANY SHOES, NO FEET

During the Second World War in Budapest, Hungary, a Fascist militia belonging to the Arrow Cross Party massacred thousands of people, many of them Jewish, along the Danube River. They instructed the people to take off their shoes and then shot them dead so that their bodies fell into the river and floated away. Heroic Swedish and Spanish leaders protected some of the people at risk and were later honored for their courageous actions. Raoul Wallenberg, in particular, is honored for his bravery in helping people escape death camps. In 2005 filmmaker Can Togay, along with artist Gyula Pauer, created a memorial by placing sixty pairs of empty shoes made of iron on the Danube embankment.

∽∽

There is something about feet that betrays the frailty of the human condition. And that frailty leads to a feeling for humankind's promise and the potential contribution of every person. To meditate on the Fascists' atrocity at the banks of the Danube is to be overwhelmed with humanity's potential for cruelty.

What looks from the outside like the empty moral character of a dark movement in human history actually reveals an absence of the emptiness that creates virtue and kindness. Those perpetrators of obscene violence were filled with the neurotic illusions of a huge complex, an agenda of massive proportions, that made them dangerous. The empty shoes point to this absence of openhearted humanity, replaced with a hard, immobile, entrenched dogma.

We contemplate those shoes, imagining lives lost, and feel for the infinite suffering of people treated without appreciation and dignity. We may think, too, of people close to us who have passed, probably without the suffering of the Danube victims, but who are nevertheless missed. I am reminded of going through my mother's closet after her passing and noticing the empty shoes there that would never again be filled.

Shoes are so mundane and apparently inconsequential as to be overlooked and taken for granted. And yet they reveal character in a way comparable to a wrinkled face. Van Gogh's painting of his own scraggly shoes immediately reminds us of his difficult life and struggles. Similar in tone is the ritual practice among some followers of Jesus to depict imprints of his feet in the ground after he ascended into heaven. I once had dinner at a convent of nuns where dessert was a ritual cake with the form of Jesus's footprints in the thick icing.

When you put your shoes on in the morning or take them off at night, you might remember the atrocity on the Danube and dedicate yourself to improving human-kind's moral development. I mean an increase in mor-als, not in moralism. Moralists are not sensitive people. They think everyone should be the same kind of person as themselves and hold the same values. They think they know everything, and, like the Nazis, they will try to clean up the world by eliminating any race or nationality they don't like. No, look at your empty shoes and remember all the people in history who have "disappeared" because for superficial reasons someone didn't like them. Empty shoes are an occasion for renewing our dedication to a free humanity.

No Porridge in the Bowl

Once upon a time, there were three bears who lived in the woods: Momma Bear, Papa Bear, and little Baby Bear. Each bear had a bowl for porridge, a chair to sit on, and a bed to sleep in, and the chairs and bowls and beds were the right size for each bear. One day, after they had made porridge and filled their bowls, they went outside while their breakfast cooled. They were quite civil, these woodsy bears.

While the bears were away, a neighbor girl named Goldilocks passed by and looked in the bears' window. She was not so well brought up. She went into the house and saw the porridge in the bowls. She tried the porridge of Papa Bear and said, "This porridge is too hot." Then she tried Momma Bear's bowl. "This porridge is too cold." Finally she tried Baby Bear's breakfast and said, "This is just right." And she ate it all up.

The girl was tired from her walk and decided to sit down for a while. First she sat in Papa Bear's chair and said, "This is too high." Then she sat in Momma Bear's chair and said, "This one is too big." Then she sat in Baby Bear's chair and said, "This one is just right." But when she sat in the little chair it broke.

Then she decided to lie down. First she lay in Papa Bear's bed. "This is too hard," she said. Then she tried Momma Bear's bed. "This one is too soft." Finally she lay down on Baby Bear's bed. "This one is just right," she said, and she fell asleep.

The bears returned from their walk and went to their porridge. "Someone's been eating my porridge," said Papa Bear. "Someone's been eating my porridge," said Momma Bear. "Someone's been eating my porridge," said Baby Bear, "and ate it all up." He stared at his empty bowl.

"Someone's been sitting in my chair," said Papa Bear. "Someone's been sitting in my chair," said Momma Bear. "Someone's been sitting in my chair, and it's all broken," said Baby Bear.

"Someone's been sleeping in my bed," said Papa Bear. "Someone's been sleeping in my bed," said Momma Bear. "Someone's been sleeping in my bed," said Baby Bear, "and there she is!" Goldilocks woke up suddenly and saw the bears looking at her, and she quickly climbed through the window and ran away.

Notice the empty bowl. Goldilocks ate up all the porridge, and Baby Bear ended up having nothing for breakfast. To grasp the meaning in this simple story, it might help to know that in its earliest versions it was not a young, golden-haired girl who trespassed on the bears' home, but a fox, specifically a vixen, a female fox. The intruder was not quite as innocent, not a young girl just passing by. Perhaps the apparent innocence of Goldilocks tells us that you have to be careful around classic innocent young women; they may hide considerable shadow under their gold-toned hair. Or less literally, in Jungian terms, Goldilocks is a soul-image, the figure who upsets the family's perfection and ruins a good day. And yet her action has a noble outcome.

In this case, the empty bowl shows that life has intruded upon the pleasant plans of an ideal family, and the baby loses things it needs: food, a place to sit, and a bed, images of home and comfort. The bears are upset to see that someone has been messing with their things, just as though a fox had entered the chicken coop.

Family perfection usually doesn't last forever, and rarely is it perfect. Something or someone comes along to spoil the preternatural peace. As a psychotherapist, I often ask a client for stories from childhood, and usually we find some element that destroys any image of complete happiness. I have told my story of a drowning, a terrible intrusion of death on a beautiful golden day. Some people have narrated a tale of a parent going into a rage or preferring a brother or sister to the person telling the story.

In another story of my own, an overwhelming desire came over me to leave home at thirteen and join a monastery with the idea of becoming a priest. It was a golden idea, but it tore me from my warm and loving family for good, at an early age, and left me in an emotionally cool and demanding life for another thirteen years, until it was too late to enjoy any of my youth with my family. I received many benefits from life as a monk, but still, the family perfection was spoiled by something that seemed to be full of sunlight. I became an adult, but ever since, I still face the empty porridge bowl, my beautiful extended family that I gave up because of some passing golden, blond ideal. Perhaps this is just growing up, leaving the glow of a good family, becoming part of a greater world. That intruder — life, anima, soul — spoiled the perfection of infantile ways but also introduced my fate and destiny. Maybe it was a necessary exchange, but it was and still is a painful one. I can still cry about it like little Baby Bear.

The psychoanalyst Bruno Bettelheim, in his cele-brated book *The Uses of Enchantment*, notes the ending in which Goldilocks just jumps away through a window. No resolution, no growing up. But in focusing on the empty bowl, I do see psychological movement in this story. The empty bowl signals a threat to Baby Bear's contented life in his family, where he is given what he needs. The appearance of Goldilocks, this nice blond girl who just happens to intrude and break up the household, changes things for the little bear, who lives in all of us. This tale happens again and again in our lives, giving us the opportunity to move on and enter more deeply and painfully into our destiny. The empty bowl spurs us onward into adult life.

Over the years as a therapist, I have found it useful for a person to tell the stories of early intruders and spoil-ers, events that upset the childhood paradise, and parents who acted out their own deprivations at a cost to their children. Sometimes it is the "golden" person, someone loved and desired, who spoils innocence and introduces maturity.

The family home is indeed a sacred place where children need protection and security and comfort and happiness. If we want a peaceful world, we have to begin with peaceful and loving families. Yet many parents are not conscious of their essential roles and how to behave in ways that give their children a solid base for life. Apparently, parenting does not come naturally, especially to people who have experienced bad parenting in their own lives — and that is most people. Not that every parent does wrong, but even small departures from emotional peace can upset children, and that upset stays with them all their lives.

We need much more education, therapy, and guidance for parents as they do their best to be with their children through challenging emotional phases and experiences that upset the children and confuse the parents. An innocent young "golden" person may come along one day and upset the family routine. This is inevitable. How to deal with upsetting developments is the task of a thoughtful parent.

Get Nothing for Nothing

Listen carefully. To the extent you give, to that extent you will be given — even more so. If you have, you will be given more. If you do not have, whatever you have you will lose.

The kingdom of God is like a person scattering seed in the earth. Night and day, whether he's asleep or awake, the seed sprouts and grows. He may not understand how. The soil makes grain all on its own — first the stalk, then the head, then the grain. When the grain is ready, he goes at it with his scythe — it's harvest time.

What is the kingdom of God like? What can I compare it to? It's like a mustard seed, the tiniest seed you can plant in the earth. Once planted, it expands and becomes the largest of all garden plants and has such large branches that birds from the sky build nests in its shade.

GOSPEL OF MARK

Last spring my wife planted tomato plants from seed. Usually we get young plants about eighteen inches tall. She kept asking me to look at the tiny sprouts, and by the end of summer we had plants full of large red tomatoes spreading out over our sun porch.

Jesus used this image of a seed to describe the kingdom, the kind of life he promoted. I see this kingdom as a new population on the planet dedicated to love and world community, cured of the human stain of narcissism and self-interest and dedicated to healing the planet and all creatures that are part of it.

It's a small thing, this idea of communal love, and yet it could transform the earth entirely. It's a seed idea, tiny and yet capable of spreading. At the end of this series of images, Jesus mentions a mustard seed, an extremely small dot of a thing, that can also grow, and grow big enough to house a flock of birds.

Amid all this talk of the smallest becoming large, Jesus says something difficult to work out in your mind: To people who have something in their lives, the kingdom will give them much more. Those who have nothing will lose whatever they have. But how can you lose what you have if what you have is nothing?

New Testament expert John Dominic Crossan, commenting on this mysterious passage, quotes the Zen poet Basho: "When you have a staff, I will give it to you. If you have no staff, I will take it away from you." Crossan explains that Jesus is speaking as radically as he can to say how the kingdom deconstructs the world as we know it. Even if you don't have anything, that will be taken from you.

This extreme wording may remind you of the end of the Heart Sutra: "absent…truly absent." As empty as can be. Even nothing has to be emptied, because you may well be tempted to make too much of your idea of emptiness. The final task is to empty your emptiness.

Jesus gives hope and promise, but he also takes away. Maybe that is why his teaching has rarely been accepted and lived out in all its radical fervor. Most people seem to say: "This teaching is important to me, but let's not go to extremes. If I really loved every human being, how could I be in business? The idea is naive."

In the Jesus kingdom, this worldly "wisdom" doesn't apply. It places a neurotic, ego-centered strain above a radical commitment to love. To be empty, religious belief can't be qualified by practical or financial concerns.

On the other hand, not having much may come with its own brand of pride: "You have it easy, but I have to struggle. I work for every little bit that I have." Maybe Jesus is saying, "In my kingdom, this new way of living, you won't be able to enjoy your neurotic nothingness any longer. Even that will be taken from you."

Jesus redefines the self. You don't become somebody at the expense of someone else. Being a self is an emptying process, not one of filling up. You will discover yourself only if you lose yourself. Padding the self, propping it up and giving it assurances, takes away from the clear, unadulterated philosophy of loving your neighbor, whoever they may be.

Emily Dickinson wrote: "I'm nobody. Who are you?" This is an excellent question. Do you define yourself by what you are or what you have or what you have accomplished? Or do you find out who you are, really, when you suffer a loss?

Just remember to keep even your loss empty. Do not glory in it. Don't "buy" anything with it. Don't look for compassion from others. Don't expect any special treatment. Don't demand a reward. If it empties you, keep that emptying empty. Don't ruin it by making your emptiness something.

MURPHY'S MIND

It is most unfortunate, but the point of this story has been reached where a justification of the expression "Murphy's mind" has to be attempted....Murphy's mind pictured itself as a large hollow sphere, hermetically closed to the universe without. This was not an impoverishment, for it excluded nothing that it did not itself contain. Nothing ever had been, was or would be in the universe outside it but was already present as virtual, or actual, or virtual rising into actual, or actual falling into virtual, in the universe inside it.

    SAMUEL BECKETT

☙❧

When he was thirty-two, Samuel Beckett, the Irish writer of plays, poems, and avant-garde novels, published a funny, philosophical, and sparkling novel called *Murphy*. He depicts Murphy's mind as a hollow sphere and describes his life as repeated attempts to be released from the burden of normal life. Murphy ties himself to his rocking chair, a metaphor for the constraints we feel when we try to live our lives freely. But Murphy the character also wants to be liberated from doing anything and going anywhere, so he takes pleasure in his rocking-chair bondage. He dies accidentally when gas explodes in his apartment, and he expressed in his will that he wanted his ashes placed in a paper bag and dumped down a toilet at the Abbey Theatre during a production. Murphy is the opposite of an ambitious, life-seeking modern person.

It may take a certain kind of sensibility, like Murphy's itself, to appreciate the humor and irony in the story, as Beckett gives us an image of the common man as not too smart. Murphy is in the tradition of the film characters Laurel and Hardy, Charlie Chaplin, and Buster Keaton, all of whom portrayed humanity with an empty mind and were prone to falls and failings. In fact, Beckett chose Buster Keaton to play the main character in Beckett's only movie, called simply *Film*. The character's task was to avoid being seen, reversing the philosophical dictum from "to be is to be seen" to "to be seen is to be." In the film, Keaton desperately tries to avoid anything that remotely looks like a pair of eyes. He flees from being a person in the world, and he doesn't want to be seen or engaged.

All the irony and humor in Beckett's portrayal of Murphy reminds us that most human beings don't reflect much and are not bothered by the intricacies of logic, history, or the accumulated wisdom of the centuries.

The common human, who is also all of us in the many moments when we are subject to our appetites and fears, is exactly Murphy, the mind a hollow sphere, a life bouncing between actuality and virtuality. Life is comic in that we survive and sometimes thrive, in spite of our basic ignorance about what we are doing and what we are here for.

This basic ignorance is much like the "sacred ignorance" that we considered in the section on Nicholas of Cusa. This is the second kind of empty mind, a positive one that knows its limits and is open to the mysteries. Most of us have both kinds of mental emptiness: We don't think enough about what our lives are all about, and we may have moments when we are open to new discoveries and revelations. In Murphy, ignorance is close to stupidity, the shadow side of mental openness. In all of us, our stupidity keeps us in touch with the deeper, more spiritually fruitful emptiness of mind.

If you have trouble with this idea, think of how stupid decisions and actions make us sink into our basic humanity. Often we may feel too clever and knowing, too certain about what we believe, understand, and act on. Often we could use some emptying out of our certainties and precious knowledge. Murphy could be our hero, someone whose mind is a blessedly empty "hollow sphere," balanced on a fulcrum between what could be and what is.

Nicholas wrote a series of short books with the general title The Idiot, a term that in his time referred to an uneducated person. Murphy is such an idiot. In Nicholas's book titled *The Idiot: On the Mind*, the uneducated person argues effectively with a distinguished professor, teaching him many things neglected in his education. Indirectly, Nicholas praises that certain brand of ignorance that is blissfully free of superior education and yet full of ordinary wisdom.

Beckett made a similar allusion in his famous play *Waiting for Godot*, in which one of the main characters takes off his hat, looks inside, and finds nothing. We can take the hat as an image for the mind. In the play the characters don't know where they are going or where they have come from. We, too, don't know where we have come from or where we are going. We live by guesses and hints. The human condition. A fundamental emptiness of mind that we perhaps defend against by accumulating information, knowledge, skills, and data that now swamp us with their size. Do we protest too much by acquiring so many facts and methods? We might take a different turn, see the wisdom in Murphy's empty mind, and live differently, perhaps more sensually and intuitively, taking more risks in a spirit of adventure, living by conjecture rather than by the illusion of superior knowledge.

NOT SPEAKING

It was Nasrudin's habit to give a talk every Friday evening at the local mosque. Hundreds of people attended because they appreciated the mullah's ability to express complex ideas in accessible and inspiring language. One Friday Nasrudin stood in front of the massive crowd and asked, "How many of you have heard me speak before? Give me a show of hands." Immediately all enthusiastically waved their hands and arms, creating an unusual commotion in the mosque.

"Well," said the mullah, "if you have all heard me before, there is no use in my speaking to you tonight." At that, he left the room and went home. The people were upset and wondered what they had done wrong.

The next Friday the crowd appeared again, and once more Nasrudin stood up before them and looked around. "How many of you have heard me speak before?" he asked. "Give me a show of hands." Well, the people were not stupid. They remembered what had happened the previous week, so spontaneously they all kept their hands down and stayed quiet.

"Well," said the mullah, "if you have never heard me speak, then you could not possibly understand what I have to say." At that, he left the mosque and went home. Again the people were disappointed.

The third week, Nasrudin came to the mosque and looked over the crowd. "How many of you have heard me speak before? Give me a show of hands." This time, half the assembled group raised their hands and half kept them down.

"Ah," said Nasrudin, "would those who have their hands up tell those who don't what I would have said?" At that, he left the mosque and went home.

Here we have a story of the speaker who did not speak and the teacher who did not teach. Emptiness of expression. Doing your job in an empty manner.

Once again, we can detect the old tradition that, as the Tao Te Ching puts it, "The person who knows doesn't speak. The person who doesn't know speaks." Or the tale of the Buddha who, when it was time for teaching, instead of speaking held up a flower. That flower became a symbol of the ineffability of the Buddha's words and the encouragement of a stunning movement toward a spiritual practice rooted in silence and contemplation, Zen Buddhism.

There is no doubt that we talk too much about things that are too mysterious to put into easy words. World history might be much more positive if 99 percent of the sermons given in all religions and spiritual traditions had not been given. All that excessive certainty, pride, attachment, competitiveness, empty speculation, sentimentality, aggression, dominance, moralism and dogmatism, thin piety, and shaky personal opinion. Maybe 1 percent of all those words spoken was really valuable.

For every word about things that matter, we need hours of contemplation and reflection. And more hours of study. Nasrudin doesn't speak because people have heard the same lessons too many times, or they have never really studied the material and wouldn't know what he was talking about. It might be better to provide an opportunity for people to talk to each other, to sort things out and come up with some provisional solutions and resolutions — their own conjectures.

Having a big, eager crowd may be a sign, anyway, that the material is too popular, not challenging enough, populist but not good for the people. The modern world seems divided between committed secularism on one side and highly emotional spiritual enthusiasm on the other. Neither offers a path to the sacred and the ultimately meaningful, to the sublime and the mysterious. One keeps the other in fashion, and neither serves insight or good living. It might be better for the spokespeople of both to stand down and go home. Maybe this is a good time to empty the churches and synagogues and mosques and sweat lodges and revival camps — workshops, too.

Language can get tired after centuries of use. After

a while the same old words continue to be said, but it becomes difficult to remember their full, vibrant meaning. For example, it's odd that Christianity is based on the simple, easy-to-understand words *love one another*. There is nothing mysterious about these words, and there is no way to argue that they are not at the very heart of Jesus's teaching. Yet people who loudly and ostentatiously profess belief in this teaching obviously do not live by the principle of love at all. You don't say, "Look, there is a follower of Jesus. He really loves people." The word *love* no longer signifies, conveys, or holds meaning. It is vacant but not empty.

It's clearly time for Christians to go home and stop meeting. They have heard the same words too many times. And Jews and Buddhists and Muslims, too. Time to go home and be silent. Let the words recover so they can once again have meaning and make a real difference.

THE SILENT FROG

The new pond,
a frog jumps in
— no sound.
RYOKAN

Here is the famous poem by Basho that inspired Ryokan's response:

Old pond,
Frog jumps in
Plop!

The original was quite empty, but the younger poet Ryokan makes it even more empty. Instead of a *plop*, we get no sound. I might prefer the translation "Silence!" In the original we could consider that it's only natural that when a frog jumps into a pond, it makes a sound like *plop*. Very Zen. But Ryokan imagines a sleeker frog, one that makes no sound when it enters the water. It's possible to be even emptier than we have always thought.

Sometimes we say of a person that they "make a splash." They are noisy with what they do, and noticeable. Other people pay attention. They can't help but notice that something has happened, someone has appeared.

One of the gifts of emptiness is to be silent. To do your job and live your life, while no one in the vicinity hears the plop of your entry on the scene. The task is its own reward, as it silently takes its place amid the torrent of events. You don't have to make a sound every time you enter the pool of life. You can live quietly but effectively.

I find that it takes some attention and awareness not to be noisy. It seems almost natural to want to be recognized and seen doing what you do. Children love to be noticed for the smallest achievements. Adults like to think they are above such childish needs, but they, too, crave attention and credit. I have always thought it important to acknowledge our need for praise and to give it to others, as well, whenever possible. We all desperately need recognition, perhaps because in the modern world it is not easy to feel seen and appreciated. As a therapist, I often give people recognition that they deserve but have been lacking. Immediately, I see them relax and feel more secure, ready for a challenge.

On the other hand, it can be deeply satisfying to do

something significant without any need for acknowledgment. I remember once when I was in maybe the fourth grade, I got a paper back from my teacher in school with an A+ on it in bright-red ink. I was bored, as usual, with school, and I thoughtlessly held the paper high above my face. The boy sitting behind me said, "We know you got an A+, You don't have to show off." I really didn't intend to broadcast my good grade, and I felt sad and embarrassed at my friend's reaction. This was a sort of reversed praise. My classmate was offended to see what he thought was me showing off. But I felt indifferent to the grade. I didn't like school. The grade meant almost nothing to me.

Sometimes you make a splash and go *plop* when you don't intend to. I am usually understated. I don't crave attention or reward. It isn't that I'm humble. As a public speaker, I show off often. But I am uncomfortable being noticed. I would rather walk through the grassy fields of life quietly, making no sound, no *plops*. I'd like to be the new frog, the one who jumps in but makes no sound. Life is easier that way.

The Lingering Grin

The Cat only grinned when it saw Alice. It looked good-natured, she thought: still it had very long claws and a great many teeth, so she felt that it ought to be treated with respect.

"Cheshire-Puss," she began, rather timidly, as she did not at all know whether it would like the name: however, it only grinned a little wider. "Come, it's pleased so far," thought Alice, and she went on. "Would you tell me, please, which way I ought to go from here?"

"That depends a good deal on where you want to get to," said the Cat.

"I don't much care where —" said Alice.

"Then it doesn't matter which way you go," said the Cat.

"— so long as I get somewhere," Alice added as an explanation.

"Oh, you're sure to do that," said the Cat, "if you only walk long enough."...

"Do you play croquet with the Queen today?"

"I should like it very much," said Alice, "but I haven't been invited yet."

"You'll see me there," said the Cat, and vanished....

She looked up, and there was the Cat again, sitting on a branch of a tree.

"Did you say 'pig,' or 'fig'?" said the Cat.

"I said 'pig,'" replied Alice; "and I wish you wouldn't keep appearing and vanishing so suddenly: you make one quite giddy!"

"All right," said the Cat; and this time it vanished quite slowly, beginning with the end of the tail, and ending with the grin, which remained some time after the rest of it had gone.

"Well! I've often seen a cat without a grin," thought Alice; "but a grin without a cat! It's the most curious thing I ever saw in all my life!"

LEWIS CARROLL

With the Cheshire Cat we behold a kind of emptiness that comes and goes and is not complete because the grin remains — if you can imagine such a thing. Lewis Carroll has a way of twisting your mind as you try to imagine as real some of the impossible things he portrays, like a grin without a body. It's a little like Alan Watts describing death as standing up and losing your lap. It's difficult to know sometimes what is present and what is merely implied.

In the story of Alice, the Cheshire Cat gives the girl directions, which adds an interesting element to this form of emptiness. We can be guided by something or someone who is there and not there, who leaves a strong impression behind but is not physically present.

Invisible presences represent an important kind of emptiness, especially in those areas that matter most, such as being guided and getting one's sense of direction. You have to be able to see the grin, so to speak, after the cat is gone. It helps to see the invisible, or at least the nearly invisible.

The cat is similar to other invisible guides like a muse, a hunch, an intuition, or a daimon. They seem present, but not fully. The daimon has been discussed for centuries and praised by W. B. Yeats, C. G. Jung, Rollo May, and James Hillman. The earliest champions of the daimon were the Greek philosophers Heraclitus and Socrates.

The daimon is an invisible presence you sense inside you or in people you encounter or just in the world. I experience my daimon almost every day, such as when I have the clear sense, as I leave my house, that I have forgotten something. Almost always I regret it if I don't pay attention to that warning. The daimon may also make its presence felt more directly and more seriously, sometimes in the form of a friend or associate. You hear the words of the person next to you, but you realize that the daimon is speaking.

It is only partly visible — a cat's grin.

Once, when I was a university professor, the chair of my department told me that the faculty had voted to deny me tenure. "You can appeal," he said immediately, as if to soften the blow. But I detected the daimon in his voice and knew there was no appeal. My life was about to head in a different direction.

Usually the daimon is not seen in the physical realm. A hunch or a sense of hesitancy comes from nowhere. The warning is intuitive, the inspiration unexpected. People say that the inspiring presence often appears in the shower, offering creative ideas not accessible at your desk or in a chair. Some say the daimon mainly warns you against making a mistake, but others know that it also inspires in a positive way. What is certain is the necessity of obedience. You must obey the daimon if you want your life to be successful. You can ignore it once in a while and even go against it on occasion. You will survive. But if you habitually oppose the daimon, your life will be a huge mistake, full of blunders. You will wonder why things didn't turn out well, while all the time the problem is that you have not obeyed the voice, equivalent to the Cheshire Cat's grin, that remains when all the visible aid has gone.

FOLLOW THE STREAM

Be soft in your practice. Think of the method as a fine silvery stream, not a raging waterfall. Follow the stream, have faith in its course. It will go its own way, meandering here, trickling there. It will find the grooves, the cracks, the crevices. Just follow it. Never let it out of your sight. It will take you.

SHENG-YEN

∽∽

"Be soft" is a good instruction, from the contemporary Zen teacher Sheng-yen, as you take up a method for spiritual and psychological well-being. Don't try too hard. Don't take it too seriously. Don't treat it as your salvation.

Being soft is a path toward emptiness. Maybe the most important lesson is not to force your own life. Don't believe that you are more intelligent and more knowing than life itself, the source of your very existence. You can follow rather than lead. You can obey rather than make demands.

Empty yourself of willfulness and intention. Look back on your life and see how you have been led toward the perfection of your calling, your innermost nature. You did not do it. Actually, you have accomplished nothing, if you have arrived anywhere at all. You have been made. Your life is a gift and a craft. You were crafted by the accumulated wisdom of insects, butterflies, and lions; trees, grasses, flowers; clouds, rain, and snow. The wisdom in all of these, inseparable from their beauty, accumulates in you. You are part of that logic, the Logos of the universe. You don't need to force it. The real skill lies in following and obeying.

If there is one lesson you need to learn, it is to follow the stream wherever it goes, meandering, getting blocked, flooding occasionally. Follow the stream that is the source of your life. Recognize the stream that has been charting your existence and creating your narrative. You are born of that stream. It is moving, not static. Unpredictable, not cemented into a doctrine or a teaching.

If someone asks you what kind of person you are, you may answer: I flow. I am not the stream of my life, but my life finds its shape as I observe and trust the stream. I don't go where I want to go; I go where the stream takes me. This obedience gives me real power. If I go where I want to go, my power will be mere control, not worth talking about.

I have developed muscles for following and obeying, not for creating and producing. I have a special vision that allows me to see the stream on occasion, so that I know where I am going. My trust in this stream gives me security and identity. I am a strong self, even though my self has not shaped my life. My affection for the stream has given my life definition and purpose. I myself am empty, empty enough to be able to follow even a trickle charting out the path.

BEING BALD

In the dawn's light I felt sad seeing the hair on my head go thin;
At twilight I felt sad seeing the hair on my head almost
    disappear.
I hated to think of the day when the last hair would fall.
Now they are all gone and it doesn't bother me.
I don't have to worry about washing and drying it.
Never again do I need a bothersome comb.
Best of all, when the weather is hot and damp
I don't have a topknot weighing down on my head.
I got rid of my soiled cloth wrap.
Now I keep cold water in a silver jar.
I pour a little of it, just a cup, on my hairless scalp.
I feel like I am baptized in the waters of the Buddha's dharma,
as I lie back and take pleasure in this cool, pleasant wash.
Now I understand why the priest finds peace
and liberates his heart by first shaving his head.
PO CHU-I

The bald head is a common sight and may require some imagination to be seen as a symbol of sacred emptiness. But Po Chu-i's classic poem from ninth-century China takes the bald head as a sign of enlightenment. He was not the first poet to do so. The Midrash, or commentary on the Bible, describes the prophet Jonah losing his hair because of the heat generated inside the belly of the whale. Jung says that the twists and turns of the hero's journey generate heat that causes the hero to lose his hair.

Po Chu-i learns that being bald is like being a monk, whose head is either tonsured (given a small bald spot), or shaved. Hair can be seen poetically as representing the products of the mind — thoughts, ideas, intentions, will. In the state of monkhood these are all given over to communal life or to the teachings. The monk is trained to empty his head of distractions and even to shave his worries.

In the poem Po Chu-i mainly discovers that life is simpler without hair, but it is also more spiritual, more like that of a bald monk. In his narrative we find another aspect of emptiness: You discover its value slowly, in stages. After a long while you may realize that it is part of the monk's life, and with it you have become more seriously spiritual.

Originally Jonah tried to flee from his instructions to help the city of Nineveh and return to his comfortable life. He resisted the will of the heavens and tried to avoid his fate by going out to sea. That is when he found himself inside the hot belly of the whale, losing his hair. His "punishment" was actually his transformation into a truly God-fearing person. He discovered the value of following a greater will, perhaps the will of life itself, to give him a meaningful direction. In that sense, we are all Jonah, tempted to exert our puny wills, learning the hard way that there is a greater design for us. We need to lose our hair, become empty-headed in that sense, bald, ready to hear the word of the heavens.

When you shed your willfulness, life becomes easier, but more importantly, you discover your monkhood. You learn the largely undiscovered truth that we are all called to be monks. Everyone. We all need a tonsure and a shave, a toning down of our many plans and wants. We would all benefit from letting life shape us into who we are. And we all need to get rid of the "hair" on our heads, the thoughts and ideas and complications and memories, that shields us from the heavens.

The Hopi Pueblo people of the Southwestern United States tell a story of how their ancestors had a little door on the top of their heads that they could open when they needed directions. A tonsure or shaved head is like that, symbolically. You have to keep your mind open to influence from the far-distant place where infinity resides. Your task is to keep your head free of distracting "hair" so you can remain open to guidance. A bald head is the sign of a superior spirituality ready to be inspired.

THE CURIOSITY SHOPPE

You will not find it on a map, but if you are patient and look carefully, you may come upon the little village of Pleasant Bay. The welcoming sign says the village was established in 1780. It lies off Route 28 about halfway between Orleans and Chatham, about midway out on the hook-shaped peninsula of Cape Cod.

My cousin Elizabeth tells a story that is hardly believable, but she tells it with such sincerity and wide-open eyes that you must take it seriously. Remember, I said that you will not find Pleasant Bay village on any map, but Elizabeth tells about her first visit to the village when she was fourteen. She was doing a school report on Squanto, the Native American who aided the European settlers when they first arrived on this continent. Squanto is known to have been active in the Pleasant Bay area and to have been buried not far from the village.

Elizabeth was staying with her aunt Kitty at the edge of Pleasant Bay and one day walked through the village's quaint streets, having an ice cream at a small stand. She noticed a special building in the center of the town's charming commercial area. The sign above the door spelled out in antique letters: CURIOSITY SHOPPE. Its windows were full of fascinating objects such as puppets, model sailboats, alarming masks, ancient books and maps, and clothing from an earlier century obviously designed for balls and important meetings. In particular she noticed an ivory-colored lace dress just her size and taste.

When she went into the shop, she immediately smelled the dank odor of antique floorboards and multi-wallpapered walls and spotted a bespectacled clerk standing behind an old-fashioned carved-wood counter. Behind the clerk and all around the thickly stocked shop, she saw more stately but quite out-of-date clothing, models of houses and bridges, gaping marionettes, and books of all conditions and subjects.

She thought she would ask the price of the dress she liked, but the clerk, a fresh-looking middle-aged woman with rosy cheeks and rosé-wine hair, was standing like a statue, looking straight ahead. "Pardon me," said Elizabeth, "but could you please tell me the price of the ivory dress in the window?"

The woman seemed to melt to life and smiled honestly at Elizabeth. "The price?" she said. "There is no price. We don't price things here. If you would like that dress, it is yours. You only have to truly want it."

"But I couldn't accept it as a gift. We don't know each other."

"But we are getting to know each other, and anyway, our store is dedicated to fulfilling desires, and we don't accept anything in return. That would ruin the spell, don't you think?"

"Oh, I do," said Elizabeth, and already the clerk was taking the dress from its place in the window and beginning to package it.

Elizabeth took the package with the adored dress home and showed it to her aunt. "How did you buy this dress?" her aunt asked. "You don't have that kind of money."

"I found it in a very nice shop in Pleasant Bay Village, where you can have what you truly desire at no cost — no money, that is."

"Pleasant Bay Village? There is no village in Pleasant Bay. You must be thinking of some other place. The place you described sounds like Chatham."

"Please come with me and I'll show you, Aunt Kitty."

So Elizabeth and her aunt walked in the same direction as Elizabeth had taken earlier, but when they got to the right spot by the bay, there was no village. Just a barren area near the beach. There was a small building that looked like an old cottage, and the shape was not unlike the curiosity shoppe Elizabeth had found earlier. But when they looked in the windows, they could see that the building was empty.

A young, light-red-haired woman was coming up from the beach, and Elizabeth thought she recognized her, a little anyway. "Is there a store in this area that sells bric-a-brac and old clothing?" Elizabeth asked her.

"Well, no," she said, "but it's funny. My brother has been thinking seriously of establishing a curiosity shoppe right here, if the area ever gets more settled. He has even thought of enlarging this old cottage."

"But now it is empty, isn't it?" It was not an idle question for Elizabeth.

"Very empty," said the young woman.

On their way home, Elizabeth's aunt said, "You must have dreamed all this."

"But I have the dress. You saw it."

"It is odd, isn't it?" her aunt said.

There is a tight connection between the kinds of emptiness that make life sweet and successful, and the mysteries that appear now and then in ordinary experience. When I went to Ireland to study philosophy when I was nineteen, shortly after arriving I walked by myself along a country road. I was charmed by the place and had always thought of Ireland as an enchanted land.

As I was walking, I spotted a clump of trees — a copse, they called it there — with stone walls near it. It was captivating, and so I left the road and walked toward it. But then a small, white-haired man approached me, as if from nowhere, and said, "Don't go near those trees. It's a fairy fort, and the fairies will certainly not have any good in mind. Stay away."

I looked at the trees more closely and turned to tell the man that I wasn't afraid, but he was no longer there. I returned to the road and kept walking. Even now I don't know if that event ever happened. Maybe it was a dream. There are times when it's difficult to know, looking back, if what you experienced was real life or a dream.

In the Pleasant Bay story, the very empty cottage in the place of the very full curiosity shoppe is a bit of a shock. The very emptiness causes us to wonder about what is real and what is imaginary. We are set on a thin line between two different realms, the world of dream and the world of fact. The story suggests that the experience of emptiness may take us to a positive place of wonder, where our life expands to the possibility of an alternative reality.

The alternative doesn't have to be fact, and Elizabeth's dress makes it clear that there are no answers to the problem of fact versus imagination. All we can do is wonder heartily and be willing to keep our minds open to alternatives. Without the empty cottage, we may not find our way to the mid-realm between fact and imagination. That would be a sad state of affairs.

THE EMPTY BUILDING

An obstetrician, an anthropologist, and a mathematician are all eating on the grass at a city park. They watch as two people enter a building on the other side of the street. A short while later three people come out.

The obstetrician says, "They must have had a child."

The anthropologist comments, "It must be a statistical error."

A few minutes go by, and the mathematician says, "If one more person goes into that building, it will be empty."

⌒

This old joke, told in many different ways, gives the illusion of philosophical mystery. It also gives us an opportunity to reflect on another quality of emptiness: It may be achieved by adding something to the situation. After all, many people get busy chanting or writing out the Heart Sutra in calligraphy, all to achieve emptiness.

Emptiness also involves an odd kind of reckoning and mathematics. Just literally taking things away doesn't always ensure emptiness. You may lead a comfortable life and have many things that please and comfort you, and yet you can be empty, especially in the sense of not being excessively attached or craving more. On the other hand, a person may not have the things they would like and may be so consumed with cravings and a strong sense of need that they are not empty at all.

Some people experience loss and expect others to care for them. Some enjoy the role of the person in need and take advantage of it. Some are simply proud of achieving what they deem emptiness in meditation and lifestyle. That pride erases the very soul of emptiness.

Emptiness is not just about adding or subtracting. The mathematician is not the expert on it. Emptiness is more an attitude and a quality of heart and character.

One day I visited my friend James Hillman at his house. We sat for a long while in the hot tub and talked dreamily about things that were personal and important to us. At one point he gestured to his chest and said with disdain, "Look, I have breasts. I can't seem to get rid of them."

James was around eighty at the time. "Why do they bother you?" I asked. "It's part of growing old." James did not look like an old man, and he had a youthful presence. "I don't think it's worth worrying about," I said. "In the things that matter, you are remarkably young." For me, his having some flab on his chest was a case of one more person going into the house and making it empty.

As I wrote in my little book of meditations on the monk's life, spiritual people are often tempted by things they don't recognize as temptations. A monk thinks that he is better than other people because he has chosen a solitary life. Thinking that you are better than others destroys emptiness. Sometimes, thinking that you are worse than others does the same thing. It might be better not to think along these lines at all.

So don't count how many nice things you own to determine whether your life is spiritually empty. Counting will not get you there. Think instead of how you feel deep down. Are you free of deep, hidden pride and striving? Are you attached to getting anywhere or being admired for what you have achieved? These are better questions when you want to assess your spiritual emptiness. But even these questions have to be empty and may not be as important as they seem.

AFTERWORD

The emptiness we are talking about rather mysteriously is both profound and simple. In spiritual matters it is the quality that arises when you are not overly attached to your beliefs and understandings, when you don't take everything literally but rather see metaphor and images, and when you live a simple life not burdened with possessions and busyness. In ordinary life, emptiness might mean clearing your desk and cleaning your house, getting rid of clutter and developing a clean sense of beauty. It could mean not filling your life with activities or people or goals. You could be empty inside and outside, in your thinking and in your lifestyle.

You might notice how you tend to fill any void that comes from loss. You may begin to eat too much, or buy things you don't need, or spend your time in crowds so that you don't have to feel your loneliness. An alternative is to glimpse the spiritual emptiness in loss and embrace it, to make something of it and let it affect your character. You probably need to empty out as much as you fill up. You don't have to take every loss as a tragedy. It may be part of the rhythm of a natural life, taking in and letting go.

Once you learn to appreciate emptiness as a positive theme in daily life, you may become a different sort of person. You may not be so anxious when losses come. You make yourself busy just to avoid facing your fate and your emotions. Busyness may be a way of avoiding real work. You don't accomplish as much when you are busy as when you take your time and focus on what needs to be done. Being busy is the opposite of being active. Being busy is full of doing with little room for reflection and conversation, which are an important part of being productive.

Now, when people meet you, they see the emptiness in your relaxed manner and in your absence of anxiety. You may look healthier and more approachable. You have empty spaces in you where people can enter. They won't feel as though they are disturbing you or interrupting your perpetual activity. This kind of emptiness can improve relationships, even marriages.

If you have rich empty oases in you, places for refreshment and pause, you can more likely enjoy a happy life. If you see a stunning mountain or lake as you travel, you can stop and take time to do nothing and look. If you see a child in need of attention, you can let go of what you are doing and be of assistance. If you need to just sit in a chair, you won't be tempted by a habit of hyperactivity to avoid the welcome rest.

Think of your life as full of parks, beaches, and mountain trails. I don't mean this literally, but as metaphors for how you spend a day. Having windows and doors in your daily schedule, you won't be confined because you will know now how important it is to cultivate emptiness.

Keep some empty easy chairs in your heart, too, so when people come along, there will be places for them to visit and be warmly received. Keep some empty spaces in your head so when a new idea appears, you can entertain it. Be empty so life can happen.

Emptiness may be a profound spiritual achievement, or it may be a quality in ordinary life. The two are related, because a simple empty hour can invite a profound spiritual realization. The Heart Sutra could be your main resource as you invite emptiness into your life — everything can be empty and therefore open to vast meaning. Even emptiness itself may be empty enough to affect your very existence.

Acknowledgments

My interest in the idea of emptiness goes back several decades, beginning with an independent study on Eastern religions with Professor Roy Amore that set me off in a mind-expanding, scholarly direction. After that Huston Smith warmly invited me to get to know Zen monks who taught me how to be empty in my everyday life. Recently my wife, Joan Hanley, got involved with a Zen community and has inspired me to see all my work as empty. My daughter, Siobhán, understands it all, always inspires me, and with her brother, Abraham Bendheim, helped me in many ways, specifically with this book.

Years ago, when I taught at a university, I used to play racquetball with Fred Streng, who wrote a classic book on emptiness. Between slams I would ask him, again and again, what "emptiness" was all about. He would usually answer, "dependent co-origination," which didn't enlighten me a great deal. He also hated to lose, and I thought his attitude lacked a degree of emptiness. But I treasured his friendship and admired his scholarship.

Others through their books have given me lessons in emptiness, notably Shunryu Suzuki, Donald Lopez, and David Chadwick. David's communications to me are always sprinkled with the emptiness of wit. In the same vein, I'd like to thank Ed Werner, who lives a life of exemplary generosity with a Zen twist. Thanks, too, to my constant friend Pat Toomay, whose emptiness seems to come from being close to the earth and open to guidance.

Finally, a thanks to Georgia Hughes and her staff at New World Library for their easy professionalism — "easy" being a mild form of emptiness. Thanks especially to Kristen Cashman, who is a writer's editor.

Each of these guides and helpers demonstrates how emptiness can make life beautiful and effective.

NOTES

p. ix   *We are surrounded by a rich and fertile mystery*: Henry David
Thoreau, *I to Myself*, ed. Jeffrey S. Cramer (New Haven, CT: Yale
University Press, 2007), 98–99.

p. 1   *Nasrudin was a spiritual leader and teacher*: The Nasrudin stories
throughout the book are adapted from Idries Shah, *Tales of the
Dervishes* (New York: Dutton, 1967); James Fadiman & Robert
Frager, *Essential Sufism* (Edison, NJ: Castle Books, 1997); and
other informal sources.

p. 5   *Harakura was the leading teacher of archery*: Adapted from a
traditional Japanese folktale.

p. 9   *A wheel's hub may have thirty spokes*: Tao Te Ching, 11, adapted
from *Tao Te Ching*, trans. Gia-Fu Feng and Jane English with
Toinette Lippe (New York: Vintage Books, 2011).

p. 17   *The kingdom is like a woman who was carrying a sack*: Adapted
from Gospel of Thomas, chapter 97.

p. 23   *A quiet night behind my grass hut*: Ryokan, in *Between the
Floating Mist: Poems of Ryokan*, trans. Dennis Maloney and Hide
Oshiro (Buffalo, NY: Springhouse Editions, 1992), n.p.

p. 27   *True practice of zazen is to sit as if drinking water*: Shunryu
Suzuki, *Zen Mind, Beginner's Mind*, ed. Trudy Dixon (New York:
Weatherhill, 1973), 108–9.

p. 33 ALGERNON: *Have you got the cucumber sandwiches*: Oscar Wilde, *The Importance of Being Earnest: A Trivial Comedy for Serious People* (London: Leonard Smithers and Co., 1912), 2, 7, 20, 21.

p. 39 *Tristan, resting trustingly on the bosom of those cosmic powers*: Joseph Campbell, *The Masks of God: Creative Mythology* (New York: Viking Press, 1968), 26–27.

p. 41 *God must, in some way or other, make room for himself*: Pierre Teilhard de Chardin, *The Divine Milieu* (New York: Harper Perennial, 1975), 87.

p. 45 *On the third day there was a wedding*: Thomas Moore, *Gospel: The Book of John*, trans. Thomas Moore (Nashville: Skylight Paths, 2018), 18–19.

p. 48 *In one of the alternative Gospels*: *Acts of John*, trans. Richard I. Pervo and Julian V. Hills (Salem, OR: Polebridge Press, 2015), 94, 97.

p. 51 *Rabbi Elimelech of Lizhensk is sitting in his carriage*: Adapted from a traditional folktale.

p. 55 *We are left as traces*: James Hillman, *The Force of Character* (1999; repr., New York: Ballantine, 2000), 202.

p. 59 *The anxiety-laden problem of what will happen*: Alan Watts, *The Way of Zen* (1957; repr., New York: Vintage, 2011), 56.

p. 63 *Early in the morning on the first day of the week*: Thomas Moore, *Gospel: The Book of Luke*, trans. Thomas Moore (Nashville, TN: Skylight Paths, 2017), 170–71.

p. 67 *You become happy when you stop trying to be happy*: Adapted from a quote commonly attributed to Zhuangzi.

p. 68 *a pheasant disappearing in the brush*: Wallace Stevens, "Adagia," II, in *Opus Posthumous* (New York: Vintage, 1989), 198.

p. 71 *You have a fishing pole so you can catch a fish*: Adapted from *The Complete Works of Chuang Tzu*, trans. Burton Watson (New York: Columbia University Press, 1968), 302.

p. 71 *took the one less traveled by*: Robert Frost, "The Road Not Taken," Poetry Foundation, accessed December 22, 2022, https://www.poetryfoundation.org/poems/44272/the-road-not-taken.

p. 73   *Were you thinking that those were the words*: Walt Whitman, "To the Sayers of Words," in *Poems by Walt Whitman*, ed. William Michael Rossetti (London: Chatto & Windus, 1901), 250.

p. 74   *James Hillman said that words are angels*: James Hillman, *Re-visioning Psychology* (New York: HarperCollins, 1975), 9.

p. 78   *Ithaca has given you the beautiful voyage*: C. P. Cavafy, *The Complete Poems of Cavafy*, trans. Rae Dalven (San Diego, CA: Harvest/Harcourt, 1976), 36–37.

p. 79   *It was time for the emperor to retire*: Adapted from a traditional Chinese folktale.

p. 83   *I became water / and saw myself / a mirage*: Binavi Badakhshâni, in *The Drunken Universe: An Anthology of Persian Sufi Poetry*, trans. Peter Lamborn Wilson and Nasrollah Pourjavady (Grand Rapids, MI: Phanes Press, 1987), 95.

p. 84   *Is it oblivion or absorption when things pass*: Thomas Wentworth Higginson, "Emily Dickinson's Letters," *Atlantic Monthly*, October 1891, https://www.theatlantic.com/magazine/archive/1891/10/emily-dickinsons-letters/306524.

p. 89   *One summer day I visited*: Teishin, "Gone Away," in *Between the Floating Mist*, n.p.

p. 93   *The Zen nun Chiyono studied Zen*: Adapted from Paul Repps, "Zen Flesh, Zen Bones," in *The World of Zen: An East-West Anthology*, ed. Nancy Wilson Ross (New York: Vintage Books, 1960), 77–78.

p. 97   *It is only when we forget all our learning*: Henry David Thoreau, journal entry, October 4, 1859, in *I to Myself: An Annotated Selection from the Journal of Henry D. Thoreau*, ed. Jeffrey S. Cramer (New Haven, CT: Yale University Press, 2007), 404.

p. 98   *Knowing not-knowing is lofty*: Lao Tzu, *Tao Te Ching*, trans. David Hinton (New York: Counterpoint, 2000), 81.

p. 101 *A little boy in China goes with his mother*: Adapted from Mu Xin, *An Empty Room*, trans. Toming Jun Liu (New York: New Directions, 2011), 7–13.

p. 103   *John Updike wrote a poignant short story*: John Updike, "You'll Never Know, Dear, How Much I Love You," in *The Early Stories: 1953–1975* (2003; repr., New York: Random House, 2004), 3–6.

p. 109   *Quan Yin / was deep into the practice of attaining wisdom*: This is the author's version of the Heart Sutra, based on reading many translations and studies of each word.

p. 115   *God would have us know*: Dietrich Bonhoeffer, letter to Eberhard Bethge, July 16, 1944, *Letters and Papers from Prison*, ed. Eberhard Bethge (New York: Collier Books, 1972), 360.

p. 119   *I followed the paths of many different teachings*: Nicholas of Cusa, adapted from Pauline Moffitt Watts, *Nicolaus Cusanus: A Fifteenth-Century Vision of Man* (Leiden: E. J. Brill, 1982), 33.

p. 123   *One day Abu Muhammad*: Adapted from Mojdeh Bayat and Mohammad Ali Jamnia, "Anecdotes of Abu Sa'id," in *Tales from the Land of the Sufis* (1994; repr., Boston: Shambhala, 2001), 42.

p. 137   *Listen carefully. To the extent you give*: Thomas Moore, *Gospel: The Book of Mark*, trans. Thomas Moore (Nashville: Skylight Paths, 2017), 23.

p. 138   *When you have a staff, I will give it to you*: John Dominic Crossan, *In Parables* (1973; repr., Sonoma, CA: Polebridge Press, 1992), 75.

p. 140   *I'm nobody. Who are you?*: Emily Dickinson, *The Complete Poems of Emily Dickinson*, ed. Thomas H. Johnson (Boston: Little, Brown, 1960), 133.

p. 141   *It is most unfortunate, but the point of this story*: Samuel Beckett, *Murphy* (New York: Grove Press, 1957), 107.

p. 149   *The new pond, / a frog jumps in / — no sound*: Ryokan, in *Between the Floating Mist*, n.p.

p. 149   *Old pond, / Frog jumps in / Plop!*: Basho, in *Between the Floating Mist*, n.p.

p. 153   *The Cat only grinned when it saw Alice*: Lewis Carroll, *The Annotated Alice*, ed. Martin Gardner (New York: Clarkson N. Potter, Inc., 1960), 89–91.

p. 157   *Be soft in your practice*: Sheng-yen, in *Essential Zen*, ed. Kazuaki

Tanahashi and Tensho David Schneider (San Francisco: Harper-SanFrancisco, 1994), 23.

p. 161   *In the dawn's light I felt sad*: Adapted from Arthur Waley, "On His Baldness," in *More Translations from the Chinese*, trans. Arthur Waley (New York: Knopf, 1919), 84.

p. 173   *my little book of meditations on the monk's life*: Thomas Moore, *Meditations: On the Monk Who Dwells in Daily Life* (New York: HarperCollins, 1994).

About the Author

Thomas Moore is the author of *Care of the Soul*, a best-seller on the *New York Times* list for almost a year. Since then he has written thirty books on soul, spirituality, and depth psychology and has traveled the world teaching and speaking, recently online and in Rome, Brazil, Argentina, Romania, Malta, Russia, Serbia, the United States, and Canada. He has also been a psychotherapist for the past forty years, influenced mainly by C. G. Jung and James Hillman, his close friend for four decades. He has degrees in music and theology and is a father and husband in a creative family that includes artist Joan Hanley, musician Siobhán Moore (aka Ajeet), and architect Abraham Bendheim. He lives in New Hampshire.